Game Set, AI

How Artificial Intelligence is Changing Tennis

By
Diana Keller

Copyright 2024 Lars Meiertoberens. All rights reserved.

No part of this book may be reproduced in any form or by any electronic or mechanical means including information storage and retrieval systems, without permission in writing from the author. The only exception is by a reviewer, who may quote short excerpts in a review.

Although the author and publisher have made every effort to ensure that the information in this book was correct at press time, the author and publisher do not assume and hereby disclaim any liability to any party for any loss, damage, or disruption caused by errors or omissions, whether such errors or omissions result from negligence, accident, or any other cause.

This publication is designed to provide accurate and authoritative information with regard to the subject matter covered. It is sold with the understanding that the publisher is not engaged in rendering professional services. If legal advice or other expert assistance is required, the services of a competent professional should be sought.

The fact that an organization or website is referred to in this work as a citation and/or a potential source of further information does not mean that the author or the publisher endorses the information the organization or website may provide or recommendations it may make.

Please remember that Internet websites listed in this work may have changed or disappeared between when this work was written and when it is read.

Game, Set, AI

How Artificial Intelligence is Changing Tennis

Table of Contents

Introduction 1

Chapter 1: The Intersection of Tennis and AI 4
    What is Artificial Intelligence? 4
    Early Uses of AI in Sports 7
    AI's Initial Steps in Tennis.. 10

Chapter 2: The Evolution of Performance Analytics..................... 14
    Fundamentals of Performance Analytics................................ 14
    AI-Driven Metrics.. 17
    Player Case Studies... 19

Chapter 3: Real-Time Match Strategies.. 23
    Predictive Modelling in Tennis 23
    AI and Shot Selection 26
    Successful Implementations 29

Chapter 4: AI-Powered Training Tools 32
    Smart Rackets.. 32
    Advanced Video Analysis 35
    Personalised Training Programs.. 38

Chapter 5: Smart Courts and Intelligent Infrastructure 41
    IoT Integration in Tennis Courts 41
    Automated Line Calling Systems.. 44
    Court Management Systems 47

Chapter 6: Wearables and Biometric Tracking.............................. 50

Types of Wearable Devices 50
Data Collection and Analysis 54
Impact on Training and Performance 57

Chapter 7: AI in Scouting and Recruitment 61
Identifying Talent with AI 61
Enhancing Scouting Reports 64
Case Studies in Successful Recruitment 67

Chapter 8: Enhancing Fan Engagement with AI 70
Interactive Platforms 70
Personalised Content 73
Virtual Reality Experiences 76

Chapter 9: The Role of AI in Injury Prevention 80
Predictive Injury Modelling 80
Real-Time Health Monitoring 83
Rehabilitation and Recovery Programs 86

Chapter 10: Optimising Coaching Strategies 89
Data-Driven Decision Making 89
Enhancing Communication with Players 92
Integrating AI in Coaching Methodologies 95

Chapter 11: AI-Driven Mental Conditioning 99
Psychological Metrics 99
Stress Management Tools 102
Case Studies in Mental Resilience 105

Chapter 12: The Future of Tennis Analytics 109
Emerging Technologies 109
Forecasting Trends 112
Potential Innovations 115

Chapter 13: Ethics and AI in Tennis 119
Data Privacy Concerns 119
Fair Play and Integrity 122

    Mitigating Unintended Consequences 125

Chapter 14: Cost Considerations and Accessibility 129
    Economic Barriers 129
    Solutions for Lowering Costs 132
    Making AI Accessible to All Levels 135

Chapter 15: Case Studies in Professional Tennis 139
    Success Stories 139
    Lessons Learned 142
    Future Applications 146

Chapter 16: AI in Amateur and Junior Tennis 149
    Tools for Beginners 149
    Development Programs 152
    Bridging the Gap to Professional Levels 155

**Chapter 17: AI's Role in Tennis Commentary
and Broadcasting** 158
    Enhancing Live Commentary 158
    Automating Highlights 161
    Personalised Viewer Experience 164

Chapter 18: Regulatory Framework and AI in Tennis 167
    Governing Bodies and Policies 167
    Ensuring Compliance 170
    Future Regulations 173

Chapter 19: Collaborations and Innovations 177
    Partnerships between Tech Companies and
    Tennis Organisations 177
    Collaborative Research Projects 180
    Grassroots Innovation Initiatives 183

Chapter 20: Myths and Realities 187
    Common Misconceptions about AI 187
    Debunking Myths 190

    Clarifying Realistic Expectations 193

Chapter 21: AI in Tennis vs Other Sports 197
    Comparative Analysis 197
    Lessons from Other Sports 200
    Unique Challenges and Opportunities 203

Chapter 22: Player Perspectives on AI 207
    Interviews with Professional Players 207
    Personal Anecdotes 210
    The Human Element in AI 213

Chapter 23: AI as a Coach's Ally 217
    Enhancing Training Sessions 217
    Real-Time Feedback 220
    Success Narratives 223

Chapter 24: Crowd-Sourced Intelligence 227
    Fan and Player Inputs 227
    Open Data Initiatives 230
    The Collective Brain of Tennis 233

Chapter 25: The Road Ahead 237
    Long-Term Vision for AI in Tennis 237
    Future Challenges 240
    Opportunities for Growth 242

Conclusion 246

Appendix A: Appendix 249

Glossary of Terms 250
    Additional Resources 251

Introduction

The world of tennis is on the cusp of a technological revolution, and at the heart of this transformation is artificial intelligence (AI). Historically, tennis relied on the intuition, skill, and strategy of its players and coaches. It was a game rooted in tradition, often resistant to change. However, the recent advent of AI technologies has begun to reshape every aspect of the sport, presenting new challenges and unprecedented opportunities.

Imagine a sport where data-driven algorithms can analyse a player's performance in real-time, suggesting strategic adjustments with pinpoint accuracy. This thrilling convergence of high-level athletics and advanced technology is not just theoretical — it's already happening. From enhancing player performance to optimising coaching strategies, AI is imbuing the game with a level of precision and insight rarely seen before.

For players, the integration of AI means access to an unparalleled level of personalised feedback. Advanced machine learning algorithms assess everything from the biomechanical subtleties of a serve to the efficiency of movement on the court. Players can refine their techniques with a level of precision once restricted to the imagination. As AI tools grow more sophisticated, they offer new dimensions of training that can elevate even amateur athletes to greater heights.

Coaches, too, are finding AI to be a formidable ally. Traditional coaching methods are being augmented with AI-powered analytics that provide insights once thought impossible. These technologies enhance decision-making by offering a deeper understanding of game dynamics and player psychology. For those committed to innovation, AI doesn't replace the rich experience of seasoned coaching; instead, it enriches it, moving the boundaries of what coaches can achieve.

Furthermore, AI's influence extends beyond the court, reshaping how the game is experienced by audiences worldwide. As spectators become more digitally engaged, AI-driven platforms offer personalised content and interactive experiences. Fans are beginning to enjoy tennis in ways previously unimaginable. Virtual reality, personalised streaming, and interactive data overlays are transforming passive viewing into an immersive adventure.

However, the integration of AI into tennis is not without its challenges. As with any technological evolution, ethical questions arise about data privacy, the potential for unintended consequences, and the integrity of the sport. Balancing these considerations will be crucial as stakeholders navigate this brave new world. Ensuring fair play and maintaining the game's competitive spirit will require thoughtful regulation and transparency.

The journey through the merging of AI and tennis is as much about embracing innovation as it is about preserving the essence of the sport. Tennis has always been about the unique blend of strength, strategy, and elegance. Incorporating AI simply adds a new layer of complexity and excitement. It's not about replacing the human element; it's about enhancing it in ways that honour the game's storied past while looking boldly towards the future.

As we delve into the intricacies of this technological transformation, it becomes clear that AI's potential to influence tennis is vast. From improving player safety with predictive injury models to revolutionising talent scouting, its applications are diverse. The coming chapters will explore how AI's evolution will likely lead to smarter competition strategies, innovative training methodologies, and ultimately, a more inclusive game that can benefit everyone from top-tier professionals to passionate amateurs.

AI in tennis is an evolving narrative. It's about taking inspiration from the confluence of technology and sport, capturing the imagination of fans, players, and coaches alike. While the road ahead is unwritten, what is certain is that AI's role in tennis is not a fleeting trend but an enduring shift. Through a combination of wisdom from the past and innovation for the future, we're poised at an exciting crossroads. Tennis, with AI by its side, will continue to thrill, challenge, and inspire in ways we've only just begun to imagine.

Chapter 1:
The Intersection of Tennis and AI

As the world of tennis meets the frontier of artificial intelligence, it's fascinating to see how tradition and technology intertwine to redefine the sport. At this juncture, AI emerges not just as a supporting player but as a pivotal force in reshaping the competitive landscape. From fine-tuning player skills to crafting superior coaching methodologies, AI influences every facet of the game. Imagine a future where algorithms delve into the depths of player performance, offering insights that were once the domain of seasoned coaches. As enthusiasts and professionals, we stand at this transformative crossroads, witnessing the melding of human intuition with computational precision. This intersection heralds a new era where potential is unharnessed, and opportunities for growth are boundless. With AI's continuous evolution, tennis is poised for a revolution, weaving its way through history with a touch of digital magic.

What is Artificial Intelligence?

At the very core of artificial intelligence (AI), there's a paradox: AI is both surprisingly elusive yet increasingly ubiquitous. It's simultaneously a subject of philosophical debates and a practical reality, changing lives and industries without us always noticing how swiftly it has permeated our world. So, what exactly is artificial intelligence? It's more than just machines performing tasks. AI refers to the development of computer systems capable of engaging in tasks traditionally requiring human intelligence, such as decision-making, visual perception, speech recognition, and language translation.

AI operates broadly through systems that perceive their environment, process data, make decisions, and act to achieve specific goals. These systems learn from experience and solve complex problems faster than any human being could. Consisting of subfields like machine learning, deep learning, natural language processing, and neural networks, AI utilises algorithms to make decisions with a level of complexity that can vary immensely.

In tennis, this vast field of AI behaves almost like an unseen coach, guiding practice sessions and matches by supplying an amalgam of data, visuals, and analyses that no human could process on their own. Imagine a system studying the strokes of a tennis player, comparing them against millions of others from history and suggesting improvements with precision. That's AI in action.

To grasp AI's essence, one must reckon with its goals: to identify patterns, learn from data, predict outcomes, and optimize results. Essentially, AI systems aim to provide solutions that are more accurate and efficient than their human counterparts—a feat achieved through processing enormous volumes of data. The ability to understand and utilize such data allows AI to exceed human abilities in specific domains. Once confined to research labs, AI now touches myriad facets of life, from virtual assistants in our homes to high-stakes industries like finance and healthcare—and, of course, sports.

One of the primary elements of AI is machine learning, which provides systems with the ability to improve learning from their experiences autonomously. In tennis, machine learning algorithms analyse match footage, identifying patterns and tactics that might escape even the most trained human eye. For coaches and players, it means an access to unparalleled insights that can be leveraged to refine skills and rethink strategies in ways never before possible.

Other essential AI components, such as natural language processing and computer vision, play critical roles in the broader AI landscape. Natural language processing enables systems to understand, interpret, and respond to human language. It isn't hard to imagine its application in creating advanced communication platforms between coaches, players, and analysts, providing real-time feedback and insights. Meanwhile, computer vision allows AI to understand images, making it a key player in video analysis technologies widely used in tennis training today.

Despite these advancements, AI is not without its challenges and limitations. Creating systems that can understand the nuances of human emotion and intuition remains astoundingly difficult. Additionally, while AI excels in processing rigid logic and data, the randomness and creativity inherent in humans—or in a highly competitive tennis match—pose significant challenges. Can AI truly understand the mental resilience required in a tiebreaker or the adrenaline rush in a five-set thriller? As it stands, bridging these elements of human experience remains an ongoing challenge in AI development.

AI's contribution to tennis is only beginning to unfold. We see its emergence in AI-powered cameras that automatically catalogue court events, smart rackets that monitor swings in real time, and sophisticated metrics that revolutionize player statistics. Yet, the future promises even more. As the technology matures, we'll likely witness broader integrations—AI systems that not only suggest game strategies but adapt intuitively, merging seamlessly with a player's on-court intuition.

AI's potential is profound, and the journey is exciting. In the context of tennis, the technology doesn't aim to usurp the human element. It endeavours to coexist, enhancing a player's natural talents and complementing the strategic acumen of coaches. AI becomes a partner in the creative dance of sport, offering a lens through which the dynamics of tennis can be observed with ever-greater clarity.

As AI continues to advance, its integration into tennis offers exciting possibilities. Imagine real-time data seamlessly flowing from courtside monitors to a player's mobile device, analyzing every shot with pinpoint accuracy. This could provide instantaneous feedback, transforming training routines and strategic planning. Visionaries in the sport are already breaking ground in this space, pushing the boundaries of what's possible and constantly redefining the player's capabilities.

However, while AI offers transformative capabilities, it comes with responsibilities that can't be ignored. Ethical considerations, privacy concerns, and the need for fairness in sport remain paramount. The seductive power of AI must be handled with care to ensure that the advancements enrich rather than overshadow the human elements so integral to tennis—passion, ingenuity, and spirit.

We're at an inflection point where AI and tennis intersect, a meeting ground of tradition and technology. This isn't merely an evolution of sport; it's a reimagination of what's attainable. As AI becomes more intertwined with tennis, it invites players, coaches, and enthusiasts to embrace a future where data-driven insights and human intuition converge to elevate the game to unexplored heights. Only time will tell the full scale of AI's impact, but its promise is one of empowerment, innovation, and a challenge to the limits heretofore laid down by human ability alone.

Early Uses of AI in Sports

The early intersection of artificial intelligence and sports was an understated revolution that laid the foundation for today's technological advancements. Interestingly, the initial uses of AI hark back to the essence of sports statistics and data analysis. Analysts began with the rudimentary task of sifting through reams of data to identify patterns and trends that could influence game strategies. Yet, the scope was limited, as computational power was in its infancy, and algorithms were basic.

One of the first sports to flirt with AI integration was baseball, famously known for its quantifiable metrics. The introduction of AI-driven statistical models helped teams evaluate player performance and optimise strategies, paving the way for more analytical and data-centric approaches to the game. This was the beginning of a profound shift, as the language of AI started entering the lexicon of sports professionals.

However, AI's early applications weren't just about data and analysis. In football, for instance, AI systems were used to create simulation models that allowed coaches to predict outcomes of various game scenarios. This provided a new lens through which to view match strategies, one that complemented the intuition and experience of seasoned coaches. Such simulations began to gain traction, offering a glimpse into a future where machines could significantly augment human decision-making.

Such enhancements were not limited to professional circles. Educational institutions quickly recognised the potential of AI in sports education, incorporating it into sports science courses. This led to a burgeoning interest among students and aspiring sports professionals, eager to leverage AI's potential to revolutionise traditional approaches.

Meanwhile, in motor racing, AI's prowess in handling complex, high-speed data computations found its niche. Advanced telemetry systems powered by AI algorithms became indispensable, providing real-time analytics far beyond what human analysts could process manually. This technology allowed teams to make nuanced adjustments to their vehicles, a game-changer that introduced a new competitive edge.

The journey didn't stop there. AI's application in sports biomechanics opened up a realm of possibilities, contributing significantly to athlete performance and injury prevention. Motion capture systems, enhanced by AI algorithms, allowed for intricate analyses of an athlete's technique and form. This level of detail was transformative, offering coaches a revolutionary way to refine technique and maximise athletic efficiency.

In tennis, the early interaction with AI mirrored similar paths seen in other sports. Initially, AI-assisted video analysis helped coaches and players dissect matches more thoroughly, identifying subtle aspects of play that might otherwise go unnoticed. These capabilities allowed for deeper insights into a player's tactics and areas for improvement. Such tools began to transform the way training sessions were conducted, blending traditional experience with cutting-edge technology.

The AI revolution in sports wasn't confined to the professional level. Grassroots initiatives leveraged AI to make sports more accessible and inclusive. Automated video capture technology, powered by AI, allowed amateur athletes to obtain professional-level insights about their performance without the prohibitive costs traditionally associated with such analysis. This democratisation of sports analytics fuelled a new kind of engagement, encouraging more participation across various age groups and skill levels.

Before the AI era, scouting and talent development heavily relied on human intuition. However, as AI technologies matured, they began to supplement these processes with data-driven precision. In football, AI systems started evaluating players based on vast amounts of match data, assisting scouts in identifying and nurturing promising talent. This multifaceted approach introduced a new level of rigour and clarity to recruitment strategies, enabling teams to make more informed decisions.

These early uses of AI in sports offer a tapestry of innovation that transcended traditional boundaries, providing a glimpse of what was possible when human expertise met technological advancement. As computational capabilities grew, so did the imagination and application of AI. It laid the groundwork for today's sophisticated systems and seamlessly integrated AI solutions that continue to redefine how sports are played, coached, and experienced around the world.

The advent of AI in sports was transformational, stirring up both excitement and scepticism within the community. The initial achievements served as a catalyst for further exploration, inspiring researchers and technologists to delve deeper into AI's potential applications. This set the stage for a technological evolution that has ultimately shaped the modern landscape of sports, creating a dynamic interplay between tradition and innovation.

AI's Initial Steps in Tennis

The integration of artificial intelligence (AI) into the realm of tennis began subtly, like the first soft strokes of dawn brushing across the sky. The sport, steeped in tradition and grace, couldn't ignore the clarion call of technology's relentless march forward. AI's foray into tennis was not a cataclysmic event; rather, it unfolded with careful deliberation, aiming to enhance the sport without overshadowing its human elements. Initially, AI found its place in aiding with mundane tasks, tirelessly working behind the scenes to transform data into gold that could be mined for insights.

During these formative years, AI's attention to tennis revolved around data aggregation and analysis. Tennis has always been a game of numbers: aces, double faults, unforced errors, and breakpoints. However, these numbers now entered a new dimension, morphing into analytics that provided a tapestry of the game's intricacies. With

AI, coaches and players could uncover patterns previously obscured by the sheer volume of data. AI, at this stage, served primarily as a statistical assistant, compiling performance metrics that could point to potential areas of improvement—an invaluable tool in the competitive arena.

Moreover, it wasn't just about processing raw numbers. AI began to unravel insights that bordered on intuitive understanding. Early AI models could analyse patterns in play that suggested when a player might benefit from being more aggressive or when a more defensive strategy was prudent. These insights, grounded in data but augmented by predictive modelling, started to campaign for recognition among traditional coaching methodologies. Coaches, some initially sceptical, found themselves leaning on AI as they balanced time-honoured expertise with new-age technology.

The scepticism was not unwarranted. The tennis community is passionate, deeply connected to its heritage, and rightly cautious of change. AI's introduction faced hurdles in the form of resistance from purists, wary of the sport's over-mechanisation. Concerns bubbled over potential depersonalisation, as AI began to influence tactics and strategies. However, advocates argued that AI was never meant to supersede human judgement but to augment it. By enhancing player understanding of their own capabilities and limitations, AI provided a platform for self-improvement.

Notable strides were made with AI's adoption by notable tournaments. Here, it wasn't just about the players; organisers found AI to be a compelling tool for improving audience experience and logistical efficiencies. Predictive analytics could, for instance, aid in predicting player matchups and outcomes, which helped in scheduling optimally to capture maximum audience engagement. Additionally, personalised viewer recommendations based on previous viewing history added a layer of interaction previously missing, drawing fans deeper into the heart of the game.

AI also began crafting its niche in player training. Early applications focused on refining techniques by capturing players' movements in precise detail through video analysis. AI-driven models could simulate match situations, providing players an opportunity to witness their performance from alternate angles. This insight allowed athletes to pivot strategies or refine techniques, shifting from instinctual responses to a more calculated approach imbued with data-backed confidence.

In parallel, AI started revolutionising the way players approached their wellness and physical maintenance. Biometric data collection became an initial step towards this futuristic vision. Monitoring a player's heart rate, stress levels, and movements provided a reservoir of information that AI could analyse to suggest recovery regimes or pre-emptive measures against injury. This opened dialogues between players and their trainers, reshaping their approach to career longevity and performance consistency.

Traditionalists feared AI would impinge on the game's soul. However, as AI began to demonstrate clear benefits without usurping the human spirit, scepticism slowly started to recede. Coaches, once tentative, grew to respect and integrate AI insights into their practice. They found the technology particularly adept at identifying weaknesses obscured even to the trained eye and providing recommendations based on vast sets of historical data and patterns.

One striking example was AI's ability to suggest real-time tactical adaptations based on analysis of live match data. By observing evolving match dynamics, AI could predict opponents' strategies and suggest optimal plays, lending a new dimension to on-court decision-making. Such capabilities highlighted AI's potential as a strategic partner amidst the high-stakes pressure of professional tennis.

As AI's role evolved, it became apparent to players and coaches alike that the technology held vast promise not just for the elite but also for every tier of the sport. As AI applications became more accessible and user-friendly, they began to democratise insights that were once a preserve of top professional circles. Aspiring players now had tools at their disposal to learn and grow, levelling the playing field in unprecedented ways.

In sum, AI's initial steps into tennis marked the beginning of a transformative journey. It eased into the sport with deference, offering enhancements without usurping the essence that defines tennis. By providing tools for improved performance analysis, training, player wellness, and spectator engagement, AI etched its role as both a partner and a catalyst, laying the groundwork for future innovations that would continue to intertwine tradition with technology.

Chapter 2:
The Evolution of Performance Analytics

As we navigate through the landscape where tennis and technology intersect, performance analytics emerges not as a mere buzzword, but as a cornerstone in the modern evolution of the sport. The paradigm shift began when technology first seeped into the courts, transforming raw data into actionable insights that empower players and coaches alike. With an ever-increasing focus on precision, artificial intelligence now unveils depths previously obscured, equipping enthusiasts with the expertise to decode every bounce and swing. In a narrative that once relied solely on intuition and experience, the evolution of performance analytics elevates understanding beyond the familiar baseline, fostering an environment where innovations continually refine and redefine competitive edge. This metamorphosis isn't just in the numbers; it's in what they enable—the strategic transformation of an athlete's potential into tangible triumphs. As we delve further into these advancements, we're not just witnessing the future; we're actively plotting its course, one algorithm at a time.

Fundamentals of Performance Analytics

The landscape of tennis has always been punctuated by the ebb and flow of technological innovation. In recent years, artificial intelligence has started leaving indelible marks on the game, augmenting traditional performance analytics. Understanding the fundamentals of performance analytics allows us to appreciate how AI has seamlessly integrated itself into the sport, transforming not only how we measure performance but also how we understand the very fabric of play.

Performance analytics in tennis is not a novel concept. Historically, it involved the manual collation of data—ace counts, unforced errors, first serve percentages. Coaches and analysts would tediously comb through match footage or painstakingly record statistics in real time, often with a degree of subjectivity. Yet, this method laid the groundwork for something far more sophisticated. As the sport embraced technology, the primacy of numbers and data-driven insights took centre stage.

One of the core components of performance analytics is the exploration of player behaviours and tendencies. By capturing and analysing in-depth data, we can discern patterns and trends that may not be visible to the naked eye. Traditional metrics like those mentioned above have served the game well, but they merely scratch the surface of what is possible when AI steps in.

AI-enhanced analytics brings an unprecedented dimension to understanding performance. It empowers analysts to derive insights from multifaceted data sources—ranging from biomechanics to environmental factors such as wind speed and court temperature. The capability to process vast amounts of data in real time is transformative, providing a richer, more holistic view of a player's performance.

Statistical analysis in tennis has leapt forward with the integration of machine learning algorithms. These algorithms sift through limitless permutations and combinations of data points, unveiling insights that might otherwise remain buried. For example, patterns in shot selection can be linked to match outcomes, offering teams invaluable predictive insights. The granular level of detail that AI can unearth equips coaches to tailor strategies and improve player performance to a degree once considered unattainable.

Moreover, AI doesn't just crunch numbers; it contextualises them. Advanced performance analytics provides dynamic interpretations of data, allowing for the crafting of narrative insights rather than just quantitative ones. This power lies in AI's ability to learn and adapt, continuously refining its models based on the latest findings in sport science and real-time data collection.

The advent of AI inevitably leads us to ask: What differentiates a marginally good performance from an excellent one? While traditional metrics provided partial answers, AI augments this understanding by taking into account parameters like a player's psychological state or adapting training loads individualised to biofeedback data. It allows the human element to be interwoven with raw numerical data, offering deeper insights into performance than numbers alone ever could.

The symbiotic relationship between AI and performance analytics extends well beyond the professional level. Amateur enthusiasts and coaches have tapped into these tools, democratising the once exclusive insights reserved for elite athletes. Practical applications in grassroots tennis ignite enthusiasm and nurture potential, providing real-time feedback and enabling everyday players to track progress—a game-changer in local clubs and academies.

The challenge, however, lies in the application of these insights. Data in itself is powerful, but the real strength is in its interpretation and action. It requires skilled coaches and analysts who can marry traditional tennis knowledge with modern technological insights to foster optimal player growth.

Ultimately, performance analytics within the realm of tennis epitomises the culmination of the past, present, and future of the sport. It synthesises classical approaches with cutting-edge technology, offering a pathway not only to peak performance but also to a deeper, richer understanding of the game. As we evolve, so too does our understanding of performance analytics. Embracing this evolution is essential for all stakeholders in tennis, from coaches and players to fans and tech developers.

While AI continues to innovate and redefine performance analytics, the principles of agility, adaptability, and holistic understanding remain key. These fundamentals ensure that tennis progresses not just as a sport but as an ever-living system intricately adapting to the pursuit of excellence.

AI-Driven Metrics

In the world of tennis, precise analysis of player performance is no longer confined to conventional statistics. As artificial intelligence (AI) matures, it's ushering in a new era of performance analytics, fostering deeper insights and offering fresh perspectives for players, coaches, and enthusiasts alike. The landscape of tennis has evolved, and AI-driven metrics stand at the forefront, transforming how performance is quantified and strategies are devised.

AI-driven metrics go beyond traditional numbers like serve speed or ace count. They're about unearthing patterns and insights that were previously invisible to the naked eye. Through advanced algorithms, AI can analyse countless variables simultaneously, creating a nuanced understanding of player performance. It's not just about what happens on the court but about why it happens. This depth of analysis paves the way for tailored training regimens, highlighting areas of improvement that might not be immediately obvious.

Take, for instance, the subtleties involved in a rally. AI can decode elements such as shot selection effectiveness, direction patterns, player footwork, and even psychological factors such as decision-making speed under pressure. By processing vast amounts of data, AI breaks down each rally into measurable components. Coaches can then use this information to tweak strategy and improve player technique in ways previously unimaginable.

Consider the application of machine learning in predicting outcomes. AI systems are trained on extensive datasets from past matches, allowing them to predict the likelihood of outcomes based on present conditions. These predictions aren't just limited to match winners. They extend to forecasting which techniques will be effective against specific opponents under varying conditions, whether it's a clay or grass court.

With AI's ability to process massive amounts of data comes the birth of what's being termed 'smart metrics'. For example, AI can evaluate the fatigue level of a player in real-time, using indicators such as movement efficiency and reaction times. In the heat of the match, such metrics enable timely interventions by coaches, helping players adjust tactics to maintain an edge over competitors.

The process of data collection and analysis is unparalleled. AI systems utilize a myriad of data sources, from high-speed cameras capturing every stroke to motion sensors in rackets and wearables. These tools provide a comprehensive dataset for AI to work with, allowing metrics to be continuously refined and evolved. This level of analytical depth would be impossible to achieve through human observation alone.

Another notable innovation is the ability to personalise metrics for individual players. AI tailors its analysis to recognise the unique style and strengths of each player, moving beyond a one-size-fits-all model. By understanding a player's specific characteristics, AI helps create bespoke training regimens that complement their natural game, ultimately enhancing performance and reducing the risk of injury.

This technology isn't limited to elite players; it's becoming increasingly accessible to amateur enthusiasts. AI-driven apps offer real-time feedback, allowing players at all levels to track their performance and receive insights that were once reserved for top professionals. This democratisation of data allows every player to benefit from the cutting-edge analysis that AI provides, levelling the playing field and providing a gateway to continuous improvement.

The intersection of AI and performance metrics is also impacting mental aspects of the game. AI systems can detect behavioural patterns that indicate mental fatigue or stress, allowing for targeted mental conditioning programs. This insight helps players maintain focus and build resilience, crucial components of modern-day professional tennis.

As AI technology evolves, so too do its applications within tennis. In just a short span, the way data is gathered and analysed has shifted dramatically. The integration of AI in performance metrics reflects this shift, introducing a dynamic and ever-evolving approach to understanding tennis. Players and coaches now have access to tools that give them an unprecedented advantage, opening new possibilities and challenging traditional methods.

The role of AI in performance analytics doesn't end with the current era. It's rapidly advancing, with the potential to redefine metrics in ways we can't yet fully imagine. Much like the game of tennis itself, always moving and adapting, AI-driven metrics ensure that the approach to excellence is continually evolving.

Player Case Studies

As we dive into the profound impact of AI on tennis, examining key player case studies provides a vivid illustration of how performance analytics has evolved. These narratives offer an illuminating window into the intimate relationship between cutting-edge technology and human potential. They capture not just numbers and algorithms but also the essence of human adaptability and the relentless pursuit of excellence.

When we consider Andy Murray's career, it's hard not to acknowledge the vital role that AI-driven performance analytics played in his resurgence after injuries. Murray's team employed a suite of advanced tools to dissect his gameplay, pinpoint weaknesses, and strategise his recovery process. By analysing his movement and biomechanics during matches, they were able to tweak his training regimens, emphasising efficiency and injury prevention. This process wasn't a solitary endeavour but a testament to the seamless integration of machine insights and human intuition. For Murray, the analytics weren't just about numbers; they became a crucial part of crafting his comeback narrative, transforming data into actionable insights.

Another striking example comes from Naomi Osaka, a player whose analytical acumen is as sharp as her gameplay. Osaka and her coaching team leveraged AI tools to enhance her preparation against opponents, developing match strategies that aligned with her strengths. By analysing massive datasets of opponents' past games, Osaka could anticipate tactics, adjust her play style, and optimise her performance. The AI's ability to scan, learn, and predict competitive behaviour offered Osaka an edge that was both strategic and psychological, reinforcing her status as a formidable force on the tennis stage.

Even the king of clay, Rafael Nadal, has embraced AI-driven performance analytics to hold his ground at the top. Despite already possessing an extraordinary array of skills, Nadal's team consistently uses data analytics to refine his gameplay and tactical decisions. In particular, they've employed AI to study court positioning and the success rates of his varied shot selections. By creating situational awareness based on data patterns, Nadal can execute plays with precision and confidence, making his strategic on-court decisions almost second nature.

For players like Maria Sharapova, who managed a successful career even as the game evolved around her, AI played a silent yet pivotal background role. As her career matured, the incorporation of performance analytics became an essential part of her training regime, assisting with fitness tracking, stress management, and tactical planning. AI was instrumental in ensuring her peak condition at major tournaments, allowing comprehensive monitoring of her physical status and match preparedness, thus prolonging her competitive grace.

Perhaps one of the more innovative case studies involves Ashleigh Barty, who managed to seamlessly switch careers from tennis to professional cricket and back to tennis. Barty's comeback to tennis wasn't just a stroke of innate talent but was deeply supported by AI-driven insights into her performance metrics. Her team expertly used AI to balance her training load, ensuring that her transition back was as smooth and effective as possible. The ability to digitally map her biomechanics and strategise her workload underpinned her remarkable return to tennis.

Then there's the promising success of younger players like Coco Gauff, whose game matured under the watchful eyes of performance analytics. At a tender age, AI helped her identify and leverage her key strengths on the court. Gauff's team worked meticulously to analyse in-game patterns using data visualisation tools, allowing her to anticipate different match scenarios and develop the astuteness of a seasoned professional. The analytics provided a robust framework for chiselling her raw potential into formidable prowess.

Furthermore, these case studies reveal how AI's evolution from rudimentary data collection to sophisticated analysis has changed its role from supportive to central within performance teams. Tennis champions increasingly rely on AI not just for reaction but for proactive strategy; transforming analytics from a reactive tool into a predictive ally.

The constant evolution in performance analytics doesn't only enhance elite players' games. Every success story resonates deeper, inspiring a new generation of players and coaches to harness AI's capabilities. Moreover, it serves as an evergreen testament to what's possible when visionary players and coaches embrace AI's transformative power.

As these case studies evidence, AI in performance analytics isn't merely an asset but a catalytic force. It's the enabler of breakthroughs, the key to once-unthinkable possibilities, opening new chapters in the book of tennis achievements. As the sport continues to evolve amidst the digital age, each case study highlights the triumphs and testaments of what happens when passionate human pursuits meet the limitless possibilities of artificial intelligence.

Chapter 3:
Real-Time Match Strategies

In the dynamic world of tennis, integrating AI into real-time match strategies is revolutionising on-court play, providing players and coaches with a cutting-edge advantage that was previously unimaginable. By merging predictive modelling capabilities with real-time data collection, AI systems can anticipate an opponent's next move and suggest optimal shot selections, transforming decision-making processes instantly. These technological marvels analyse vast datasets, offering insights faster than the human mind can comprehend, allowing for swift strategic shifts that are crucial in high-stakes matches. Successful implementations of such technologies have already begun to alter the landscape of professional tennis, where the difference between winning and losing hinges on split-second decisions. As AI tools become more adaptive and responsive, they empower players not just to react but to strategise proactively, crafting gameplay that is as intelligent as it is intuitive. Thus, AI is not merely a technological leap forward; it's reshaping the fabric of the sport, making each match a thrilling interplay of human skill and digital acumen.

Predictive Modelling in Tennis

Imagine stepping onto a tennis court, where every volley, serve, and spin can be predicted with mathematical precision. This isn't just a futuristic fantasy—it's the reality of predictive modelling in tennis. As artificial intelligence continues to permeate the sport, it's reshaping how players and coaches approach matches, providing a competitive edge through data-driven insights.

At the heart of predictive modelling lies the concept of anticipation. Tennis is a sport where seconds matter; the ability to foresee an opponent's next move can dramatically shift the game's outcome. Through AI, vast amounts of data are analysed to identify patterns, tendencies, and outcomes, allowing players and coaches to strategise with unparalleled accuracy. Historical match data, weather conditions, and even slight variations in player performance are fed into sophisticated algorithms. The result? Predictive models that suggest the possible trajectories of a match, offering insights into opponents' likely strategies and weaknesses.

Consider the application of predictive modelling in player preparation. Before a big match, a player can use AI-generated models to review their opponent's past performances. These models can reveal, with surprising specificity, how that opponent responds under pressure or prefers to open a rally. By understanding such nuances, players can train specifically to counteract these tendencies, turning AI predictions into actionable strategies on the court.

Coaches also benefit enormously from these advancements. Instead of relying solely on intuition or anecdotal evidence, they can base their strategies on hard data. For instance, if an opponent has a low success rate in returning high-spin serves under windy conditions, predictive modelling can suggest employing that very serve as a primary tactic. This shifts the role of a coach from merely observing and instructing to one of a data strategist, armed with insights to optimise player performance. Such is the power of AI in transforming coaching methodologies.

The technology behind predictive modelling is as fascinating as it is complex. At its core, machine learning algorithms drive these models, absorbing endless streams of data—from Hawkeye systems capturing intricate ball movements to sensors that measure player biomechanics. As these systems learn across thousands of matches, they refine their predictions, akin to how a grandmaster gradually understands the subtleties of a chessboard.

Of course, predictive modelling is not without its challenges. The precision of predictions depends significantly on the quality and quantity of data available. In this pursuit, the integration of multiple data sources becomes crucial, requiring a seamless confluence of technology and sport. Future advances can broaden the scope of data inputs, incorporating aspects like player mood or energy levels, creating a more holistic view of the game dynamics.

Moreover, this predictive capability is reshaping the mental landscape of tennis. Players, armed with insights about their own game and their adversaries, gain psychological advantage. This isn't just about physical prowess anymore—it's about playing a smarter game. Competitors who effectively leverage predictive insights can dictate the flow of play, knowing when to push aggressively or hold back, thus gaining a substantial mental edge.

While the technological sophistication of predictive modelling is remarkable, perhaps its most revolutionary aspect is accessibility. These tools are no longer the exclusive domain of top-tier professionals with extensive resources. As technology evolves and costs decrease, predictive analytics become accessible to coaches and players at all levels, democratising the benefits of AI-driven insights. This opens up enormous possibilities for player development and competitive fairness across the tennis world.

The implications of predictive modelling extend beyond individual matches. At a macro level, it offers insights into broader trends and shifts within the sport itself, helping tennis federations and organisers devise strategies for player development and competition structures.

As AI continues to harvest a wealth of data, its potential to forecast the evolution of tennis strategy on a global scale is indeed exciting.

Yet, amidst this wave of data and technological prowess, it's essential to remember the human element that remains at the core of any sport. While AI and predictive models provide significant advantages, the unpredictable nature of human performance can often outwit even the most sophisticated algorithms. The beauty of tennis lies in those unexpected moments of brilliance and resilience, where the heart and mind converge in a dance of grit and inspiration. Predictive modelling brings new dimensions to this dance, but the essence of the game—its spontaneity and raw human emotion—remains untouched.

In closing, the integration of predictive modelling in tennis heralds a new era of strategic sophistication. It empowers players and coaches to craft strategies with previously unimaginable precision, thereby raising the level of competition. As AI technology evolves, its role in shaping the future of tennis will only grow, transforming players into smarter, more intuitive athletes. For the tennis community, embracing these technological tools without abandoning the soul of the sport presents both a challenge and an exhilarating opportunity.

AI and Shot Selection

In the high-stakes world of professional tennis, the ability to make split-second decisions on shot selection can mean the difference between victory and defeat. This is where artificial intelligence (AI) steps in to transform the game. AI leverages vast amounts of data to optimise shot choices, offering players a competitive edge by providing insights that were previously unimaginable. It's no longer merely about the player's intuition or experience but about augmenting these with precise, data-driven intelligence.

Shot selection is a dynamic interplay of strategy, skill, and psychological warfare—a complex mix that AI can help untangle. AI technology can analyse an opponent's weaknesses and predict their likely responses, allowing players to exploit these with pinpoint accuracy. By examining historical match data, AI systems can identify patterns and suggest plays with higher success probabilities, essentially acting as a tactical advisor during live matches.

Imagine a scenario where a player faces the daunting challenge of a tie-breaker. Traditional coaching might involve drilling specific strategies into the player's mind, hoping they remember in the heat of the moment. In contrast, AI can feed real-time analytical data suggesting the most effective serve or rally strategy based on countless past encounters. This augments the player's natural decision-making process, turning pressure into opportunity.

One of the transformative aspects of AI in shot selection is its capability to integrate with existing technologies. With wearable sensors and smart rackets, AI can offer instantaneous feedback on the efficacy of a chosen shot. Did the backhand slice have the desired spin? Was the forehand drive powerful enough to be a winner? Such queries can be evaluated in real-time, allowing for mid-match adjustments and improvements that can turn the overall tide.

Yet, AI's contributions go beyond reactive analysis. Before the first serve, players can engage in virtual simulations orchestrated by AI, designed to acclimate them to different styles of play and conditions. This preparatory work includes analysing massive datasets from past encounters, giving players insights into what strategies might work best against specific opponents. As players step onto the court, they're armed not only with their own skill but also with a repository of tactical wisdom culled from thousands of matches.

The potential of AI in shot selection would be constrained without considering the human element. Tennis isn't played in a vacuum but in an environment filled with myriad psychological factors. AI must adapt to these, recognising when a player is mentally fatigued or showing signs of emotional stress. Subtle cues, such as shifts in a player's on-court movement patterns or changes in their shot execution speed, provide AI with data to suggest the most appropriate shot choice at that exact moment.

Additionally, AI's role is not solely restricted to predicting the opponent's gameplay. It also involves understanding a player's own style and preferences, the subconscious nuances that define a champion's temperament. This adaptability allows AI to forge strategies that are personalised, optimising every aspect of a player's performance based on their individual strengths and weaknesses.

There are, understandably, challenges and reservations. Some purists might argue that over-reliance on AI could undermine the artistry and instinct that are hallmarks of great tennis. While it's true that AI introduces a level of calculation previously unseen, it should be viewed as an augmentative tool rather than a replacement for a player's inherent skills. By mastering this new dimension, players can not only match the prowess of opponents but also elevate their own game to new heights.

The development of AI algorithms for tennis shot selection is an ongoing evolution, with engineers and data scientists continuously refining the models to accommodate various surfaces, environmental conditions, and emerging playstyles. This constant iteration ensures that the AI remains a living entity capable of adapting to the sport's ever-changing landscape.

Moreover, the grounding principles of AI in shot selection—pattern recognition, predictive analytics, and machine learning—are laying the foundation for a broader revolution across the sport. As these technologies become increasingly sophisticated, they promise to extend beyond the upper echelons of professional play and become accessible to weekend warriors and aspiring juniors alike, democratising strategy and skill enhancement.

Ultimately, AI's integration into shot selection represents a fusion of tradition with technology. It's about preserving the spirit of tennis while embracing the innovations that can elevate it. Players, coaches, and enthusiasts alike are venturing into a new era of the game where the meticulous brilliance of AI complements the raw, pulsating excitement of human endeavour on the court.

Successful Implementations

In the rapidly evolving world of tennis, the integration of AI in real-time match strategies has been nothing short of transformative. Take, for example, the use of AI in predictive analytics during matches. Coaches and analysts now harness the power of machine learning algorithms to assess vast amounts of historical match data. These algorithms predict likely outcomes based on current match conditions, enabling real-time strategic adjustments that could tilt the scale in favour of a player or team. This level of insight was once considered unattainable, limited by traditional analytical methods and human cognition.

The sophistication of AI systems in shot selection has introduced a new dimension to match tactics. Consider the case where AI models are utilized not just to analyze past performances but to simulate potential scenarios. These simulations assist players in selecting the most statistically advantageous shots, enhancing their play and confounding competitors. AI's capability to process visual and statistical data concurrently leads to decisions that are not only quick but optimally aligned with real-time match dynamics.

A noteworthy success story emerged from the partnerships between elite tennis academies and AI firms. These collaborations have fostered innovative platforms that offer nuanced insights into player performance during high-stakes matches. Such platforms analyze a player's in-match behaviour, spotting opportunities to exploit opponents' weaknesses or adjust their tactics for better defensive or offensive play. This kind of real-time adaptability, embracing the power of AI, is invaluable, especially in situations where the margin for error is extremely narrow.

Another successful integration of AI in match strategy is found in its application for live match commentary and tactical insights. Commentators equipped with AI tools can delve into in-depth analysis and deliver enriched viewing experiences for audiences. These tools provide statistical substantiation to the tactics being employed on the court, offering spectators a deeper understanding of a match's unfolding strategy. As a result, fans are more engaged, turning watching tennis into a more interactive experience.

Beyond professional realms, AI-driven real-time strategies have seen successful implementations in grassroots tennis. AI technology is being leveraged to create applications that offer instant feedback to amateur players on their shot choices and tactical positioning. These solutions make use of the same principles as their professional counterparts, but they are streamlined for accessibility and ease of use by players at all levels. By fostering tactical understanding and adaptation, AI aids in democratizing a level of strategic thinking that was previously inaccessible to non-professionals.

Moreover, AI technologies have shown proficiency in simulating different playing conditions. This aspect is particularly useful in tournaments, where players face opponents they have never competed against in varying conditions. AI predictive modelling enables players to anticipate how their own play might need to adapt or how their opponent's familiar strategies might be altered by unique conditions. This ability to preempt and strategize based on simulations ensures that players are not just reacting but are proactively managing match conditions to their advantage.

A compelling instance of successful implementation is in the area of digitally enhanced tactical coaching sessions. Here, AI has enabled coaches and players to collaboratively refine strategies well ahead of matches. By simulating a wide array of possible in-game scenarios, AI tools allow for extensive pre-match tactical planning and player conditioning. Players can mentally rehearse and be ready for different configurations of play, giving them an edge that is both psychological and strategic.

However, while AI advances in real-time match strategy are laudable, it is essential to acknowledge the ongoing challenge of ensuring these technologies remain accessible and comprehensible to all levels of play. Not every player or coach might possess the necessary technical expertise to optimise these advanced solutions, highlighting an area for further development to ensure that AI's benefits can be universally harnessed in the tennis community.

Lastly, as technology continues to penetrate the strategic aspects of tennis, the sport's traditionalist elements are being cautiously woven with modern technological advancements. The integration of AI into strategic decisions needs to be implemented in ways that respect the game's heritage while celebrating its innovative potential. It's a delicate balance, but where successfully implemented, the results speak for themselves: the enhancement of player performance, the evolution of game strategies, and the overall revolutionising of the tennis experience—driven by the power of AI.

Chapter 4:
AI-Powered Training Tools

As tennis continues to embrace the digital transformation, AI-powered training tools are at the forefront of this revolution, empowering athletes and coaches alike. Smart rackets equipped with sensors analyse every stroke, providing real-time feedback that allows players to refine their technique with pinpoint accuracy. Meanwhile, advanced video analysis tools break down player movements with surgical precision, uncovering insights that were once the domain of only the most perceptive coaches. These innovations make personalised training programs possible, customising regimens to fit the specific needs and goals of each athlete. By integrating these AI tools into their routines, players can optimise performance, hone their skills, and elevate their game to new heights, all the while fostering a deeper connection between human intuition and technological prowess. The result is not just an enhancement in performance but a transformation, as athletes gain the edge needed to excel in today's competitive landscape.

Smart Rackets

The tennis racket is no longer just a tool to hit the ball; it's evolving into an intelligent device that can revolutionise the way players train, compete, and even understand the game. Smart rackets are the latest frontier in AI-powered training tools, offering advancements that blend seamlessly with both traditional and cutting-edge techniques. As players search for ways to optimise their performance, smart rackets provide a valuable resource equipped with sensors that collect data on every detail of a stroke.

These innovative rackets come embedded with sensors that capture an array of data, from swing speed to ball contact spin. They then analyse this information using complex algorithms to offer real-time insights that players can use to refine their skills. The data is not just numbers—it's a breakdown of one's personal playing style and an exploration into areas for improvement. This feedback is instantaneous, allowing players to make adjustments on the fly, rather than waiting for post-match analysis.

One might wonder, how exactly do these smart rackets work? Typically, they're equipped with Bluetooth technology that syncs data to an app on a smartphone or tablet. This interface then visualises the data in a readable form, offering guidance on shot accuracy, footwork dynamics, and even fatigue levels. Players can see their stats instantly after a session, adjusting their techniques and strategies based on empirical data rather than subjective assessment.

Imagine being able to track not only how many forehands you hit during a practice session, but also how efficient each one was. Smart rackets take tennis analytics to the next level by phrasing performance data in terms the player can actually use. For instance, a player struggling with inconsistent backhand shots can use the insights derived to tweak minor details in their grip or stance, consequently turning a weakness into a strength.

Additionally, smart rackets hold the keys to tailoring training programmes to specific needs. Instead of adopting a one-size-fits-all regimen, players can devise targeted drills based on real-time data analytics. Coaches, too, can benefit significantly; using the data generated, they can tailor their instruction more accurately to the player's unique style. This level of personalisation can be pivotal in a player's journey from a weekend warrior to a competitive athlete.

What makes smart rackets truly revolutionary is their ability to bridge the gap between novice and seasoned pros. For beginners, interpreting the data allows them to develop good habits early on, setting a solid foundation for future skills. They can practice with the confidence that they're using data-driven methods to improve, which only boosts their motivation. For professionals, it means having the luxury to dig deeper into their performance metrics, scrutinising each aspect to maintain a competitive edge over rivals.

Yet, the appeal of smart rackets isn't solely technical. They also inject an element of fun and curiosity into training and gameplay. By gamifying practice sessions, players can set goals based on data benchmarks, transforming the training process into an engaging and competitive scene. Imagine a player working tirelessly to achieve their first 'perfect ten' in swing speed, their journey logged and guided by the smart racket—a feat celebrated digitally in much the same way as a high score on one's favourite video game.

Moreover, smart rackets lend themselves well to the social dimension of tennis, allowing players to share data, challenge others, and even form networks based on skill analytics. They foster a sense of community and friendly competition, where exchanging insights becomes commonplace among amateur clubs and professional circuits alike. The data-driven verdicts pave the way for insightful conversation and collaboration, inspiring players to continually push the boundaries of their potential.

However, it's essential to consider the balance between technology and traditional skills. Some purists argue that reliance on data may overshadow innate talents, but the true synergy lies in blending both to create a new horizon for excellence. As the debate continues, smart rackets already have their foot on the modern tennis court, performing invaluable roles in nurturing and developing players.

Smart rackets epitomise the innovation stride AI is making in sports. They harmonise seamlessly with AI-powered training tools, such as advanced video analysis and personalised programmes, forming a cohesive ecosystem. The data and insights gained from smart rackets can inform broader strategies for player development, enriching the entire spectrum of AI-driven sport science.

With technological advancements evolving rapidly, the world of smart rackets is inspiring. As they continue to evolve, these rackets may feature more advanced AI capabilities, potentially providing players with predictive insights or even real-time coaching advice. Picture a game where every tactical decision is underpinned by AI analyses tailored to real-time, on-court conditions. The potential is as vast as the sport itself, as smart rackets can redefine what's possible and transform the landscape of tennis training forever.

Advanced Video Analysis

The transformation of tennis through AI is perhaps most vividly seen in **advanced video analysis**, a tool that's redefining training and performance evaluation. In the realm of player development, the ability to scrutinise every nuance of a player's movements and techniques marks a significant departure from traditional coaching methods. What was once reliant on the trained eye of a seasoned coach can now be augmented with a meticulous digital overview. This fusion of human intuition and machine precision leads to not just better players, but smarter coaching too.

AI-powered video analysis provides a comprehensive suite of metrics that can be used to assess matches, practices, and training regimes. By capturing every frame and translating it into quantifiable data, coaches and players are presented with a new vista of information they can utilise to their advantage. From footwork patterns to stroke mechanics, and even emotive cues like body language under pressure, AI distills video footage into actionable insights that were previously unattainable.

One of the most profound benefits of advanced video analysis is the ability to understand an athlete's biomechanics in granular detail. This factor contributes not only to performance enhancement but also to injury prevention. By identifying inefficiencies or potentially harmful techniques, adjustments can be made in real-time, safeguarding player health and contributing to career longevity. It's almost like having an X-ray of one's technique, providing clarity and focus on areas of improvement.

Moreover, with AI systems capable of learning and adapting, over time they become attuned to the intricacies of each individual player. This personalisation extends beyond mere technique adjustments; it encompasses the psychological aspects of sport too. How does a player respond to specific stressors? Do performances falter in high-stakes situations? With AI dissecting these behavioural patterns, psychological training can be tailored to bolster mental fortitude alongside physical prowess.

AI doesn't just stop at individual performance; its impact is significant at the game strategy level. Pre-match preparations are now bolstered by detailed analysis of opponents' past matches, revealing weaknesses and tendencies that can be exploited in a game plan. Coaches can construct strategies that are not only tailored to the player's strengths but also precise in targeting the opponent's vulnerabilities. This strategic advantage is akin to having a chess game mapped out several moves ahead.

The beauty of this AI-driven evolution lies in its accessibility. While advanced technology once remained the purview of elite competitors, increasingly diverse and cost-efficient tools are available to clubs and players at all levels. Whether it's through smartphone apps or high-end bespoke systems, the technology is democratising access to high-quality performance analysis that was once reserved for the top echelons of the sport.

Looking at the broader landscape, AI-enhanced video analysis holds a promise beyond mere data collection. It fosters an interactive environment that simultaneously empowers coaches and players. By providing a visual and data-driven context, it bridges communication gaps and ensures that instructional advice is immediately applicable. This dynamic mode of learning fuels engagement and instills confidence, knowing that every adjustment is backed by empirical evidence.

These innovations also bring an educational component to tennis, nurturing not just today's stars but future generations of players. Youth academies and training camps are integrating AI into their curriculums, teaching young enthusiasts the value of data literacy alongside technical ability. By instilling an analytical approach early, these players are better equipped to self-correct and evolve throughout their careers, fostering a new breed of tech-savvy athletes.

What's more, the ripple effects of advanced video analysis extend beyond player and coach. Fans and commentators gain enriched insights, enhancing their viewing experience and engagement with the sport. Detailed analysis of key moments and comprehensive breakdowns of complex plays transform spectators from passive viewers into active participants in the game's narrative.

Ultimately, as AI continues to evolve, the potential applications in video analysis will only expand. With machine learning models becoming ever more sophisticated, they will offer even deeper insights and more nuanced feedback, allowing players and coaches to not only reach their potential but redefine it continuously. The synergy of human creativity and AI's computational muscle is reshaping the possibilities within the tennis arena and beyond.

Personalised Training Programs

In the fast-paced world of tennis, one-size-fits-all training programs are no longer sufficient to meet the diverse needs of athletes at various skill levels. Enter AI-powered personalised training programs—tailored regimens designed to cater to a player's unique strengths and weaknesses. These cutting-edge programs harness the power of artificial intelligence to analyse vast amounts of data, adapting to each player's evolving goals, and providing the precise feedback necessary for maximising performance.

Imagine a young athlete hoping to emulate her tennis idol. With an AI-driven training program, her aspirations are no longer just a distant dream. Through advanced algorithms, AI can identify areas where she excels and pinpoint aspects that need improvement. Such precision ensures that each training session is optimally structured, focusing on her specific needs rather than generic drills. As the athlete progresses, the AI continuously adjusts the program, pushing her towards her peak potential.

The process is remarkably dynamic. Modern AI systems can analyse metrics from the player's performance data, whether derived from match play, practice sessions, or simulation environments. Using insights from technologies like smart rackets or wearables, AI can track everything from swing speed and spin rate to footwork patterns. This data is translated into actionable insights that shape the athlete's training routine, making it far more efficient and tailored.

An important facet of personalised training powered by AI is the integration of advanced video analysis. While coaches have traditionally relied on manual video review to assess player techniques, AI offers a far more insightful solution. It can automatically break down video footage and assess each movement with astonishing detail. This not only saves time but also highlights aspects that might be overlooked by the human eye. Coaches can then use this granular analysis to make more informed decisions about technique adjustments.

AI does not function in isolation; it is a robust toolset that empowers coaches and players alike. Machine learning algorithms can predict outcomes and recommend interventions, yet they also encourage a collaborative approach. Coaches, with their expertise and intuition, are essential in interpreting the data AI generates. They can offer nuanced insights and context that complement AI findings, creating a harmonious blend of human judgment and machine precision.

In an era where mental conditioning is as crucial as physical training, AI doesn't falter. It can suggest routines for mental resilience and stress management, drawing from psychological metrics captured during training. Such insights are invaluable, supporting players to not only perform better but also maintain optimal mindsets. Through personalised feedback loops, athletes can address mental barriers that might hinder performance, thus providing a truly holistic training regime.

The ability of AI to individualise training also extends to scheduling. With knowledge of an athlete's peak performance times, rest patterns, and fatigue levels, AI can suggest optimal training windows. These suggestions help players achieve peak physical condition without overtraining or risking injury. The balance it provides is crucial in preventing burnout and extending the athlete's prime years.

For tennis enthusiasts or sports professionals witnessing this transformation, the future looks exceedingly promising. AI's role in devising bespoke training programs signifies a radical shift in how players approach their development. By offering these tailored experiences, athletes are more likely to remain engaged and motivated, seeing tangible improvements that correlate directly with the efforts invested.

Yet, the personalisation of training goes beyond the court. AI tools can guide athletes on nutritional plans tailored to their specific physiological profiles, ensuring they get the right fuel for performance and recovery. This comprehensive approach signifies a move towards an all-encompassing support system, where every aspect of an athlete's lifestyle is considered, empowering them to achieve their best not just on the court, but off it too.

Despite the transformative benefits, challenges remain in ensuring equitable access to such advanced technologies. While top-tier players and academies may readily adopt these tools, it's crucial that artificial intelligence becomes accessible across all levels of the sport. Facilitating broader access will democratise tennis training, allowing players from diverse backgrounds to benefit from AI-driven personalisation.

In closing, AI-powered personalised training programs are revolutionising tennis in unprecedented ways. They stand at the intersection of innovation and intuition, driving personalised development paths that are as unique as the athletes themselves. As AI continues to evolve, its capacity to fine-tune and personalise will undoubtedly propel the sport to new heights, creating champions who are not just the best in the present, but are well-prepared for the challenges of the future.

Chapter 5: Smart Courts and Intelligent Infrastructure

Imagine stepping onto a tennis court that's more than just a playing surface; it's a hub of advanced technology. Smart courts and intelligent infrastructure are transforming these spaces into dynamic environments that enhance both playing and spectating. Through the integration of the Internet of Things (IoT), tennis courts now boast sensors and connected devices that collect real-time data to improve player performance, track ball speed and trajectory, and even manage the venue's operational efficiency. Automated line calling systems are raising the bar for accuracy in officiating while reducing human error, providing players and fans alike with more confidence in the fairness of each game. These innovations extend to court management systems, streamlining everything from scheduling games to maintaining optimum playing conditions. As artificial intelligence weaves its way into these foundational aspects of tennis, the game is becoming smarter and more enjoyable for everyone involved, blending tradition with innovation in an exciting new chapter for the sport.

IoT Integration in Tennis Courts

In the digital era, tennis courts are no longer just static spaces where matches unfold. They're evolving into dynamic, interconnected environments thanks to the Internet of Things (IoT). IoT integration in tennis courts introduces an infrastructure that communicates in real-time, revolutionising both player experience and court management. This fusion of technology and athleticism offers an intelligent framework that continually gathers and processes data, turning each court into a hub of innovation and insight.

The integration begins with sensors embedded throughout the court. These sensors track ball speed, trajectory, and bounce location, providing instant feedback for coaches and players. Imagine a scenario where, as a player serves, data regarding the spin, speed, and placement of the ball pops up on a coach's handheld device. This immediate access to detailed statistics empowers players to make informed decisions and adjust strategies mid-match, elevating their game to new heights.

IoT-enabled systems do more than track the movement of the ball; they also monitor environmental conditions. Temperature, humidity, and wind speed can all impact play, and having precise data on these variables allows players to fine-tune their techniques accordingly. Knowing how crosswinds might affect different strokes can lead to tactical adjustments that separate victory from defeat. This kind of data-driven adaptability represents a significant leap forward in performance analytics.

Beyond player performance, IoT integration facilitates smarter court management. Automated scheduling systems optimise the use of facilities by tracking usage patterns and adjusting availability based on demand. For example, a sensor-equipped court can automatically signal maintenance needs, such as surface wear or net tension adjustments, ensuring the playing environment is always in peak condition. Courts equipped with IoT technology can also control energy usage more efficiently, adjusting lighting or heating based on court occupancy, thus reducing operational costs over time.

From a player's perspective, IoT makes the tennis experience more engaging and personalised. Connected apps can track individual progress, providing historical data and performance trends over time. Players can access personalised dashboards where insights from past matches and training sessions are displayed. The ability to analyse this data individually ensures that athletes aren't just keeping pace with their peers, but are also continually improving their unique play styles.

Interactive features extend even further to spectator engagement. Smart seats equipped with sensors can offer immediate feedback on seating comfort, send live match statistics, or allow fans to order refreshments without missing a second of the action. This elevated fan experience forges a deeper connection between the audience and the sport, encouraging greater participation and enthusiasm.

On a larger scale, IoT integration on tennis courts is laying the groundwork for grassroots development. Local clubs equipped with these technologies can offer a level of sophistication previously reserved for elite centres. This democratisation of technology provides aspiring players at all levels with the tools to compete and improve in ways once thought impossible outside of professional environments.

The integration of IoT isn't without its challenges. Ensuring data privacy and security is paramount as more sensitive information—about player habits, health data, and private sessions—flows between devices. Creating robust encryption protocols and secure networks will be key to maintaining trust in these systems. Additionally, the infrastructure costs of implementing IoT at scale require careful planning and considerable investment, though the long-term benefits often outweigh the initial expenditure.

As we gaze into the future, IoT's role in tennis is only expected to grow. Emerging technologies will build upon the foundations of current IoT systems, promising even more sophisticated, interconnected networks. With the potential for real-time data becoming ever more intricate and actionable, the boundary between technology and human potential will continue to blur, leading us to reimagine what's possible on the tennis court.

IoT integration in tennis courts is an exhilarating development, drawing us closer to a future where data calls the plays and every volley echoes with strategic intent. It's not just about chasing the next point, but about playing the game in a smarter, more engaging way. Through insights, efficiency, and enhanced experiences, the game is evolving—and players, coaches, and fans worldwide are all part of this exciting transformation.

Automated Line Calling Systems

In recent years, tennis has embraced technology to a degree once unimaginable, and nowhere is this clearer than in the adoption of automated line calling systems. With the frenetic pace of high-level tennis and the often-narrow margins determining a ball's fate—whether in or out—precision in line calls has become crucial. Technology-driven line calling systems provide not only accuracy but also objectivity, mitigating potential disputes and ensuring a fair game.

Traditionally, human line judges have evaluated whether a ball lands within the boundaries of the court. Despite their skill, even the sharpest eyes can falter under pressure. Automated systems, however, utilise an array of cameras and sensors that can analyse ball trajectory in real-time, offering rulings with pinpoint precision. These systems operate by capturing images or video of each shot and using sophisticated algorithms to assess the ball's position relative to the court's lines.

Arguably, the most celebrated of these systems is Hawk-Eye, which has become a staple in tennis tournaments worldwide. Hawk-Eye tracks the ball's path via a network of high-speed cameras positioned around the court. It gathers data that's quickly processed to render a virtual image of the ball's trajectory, helping umpires make informed decisions. The system has gained the trust of the tennis community and revolutionised the way contentious points are settled; players can challenge a call, and within seconds, the system provides a clear, visual representation of where the ball landed.

But the journey towards fully automated line calling systems wasn't without hurdles. Initial scepticism revolved around the accuracy and reliability of such systems. Could technology truly emulate, or even surpass, the nuanced judgements of seasoned line judges? Over time, through rigorous testing and continual enhancements, these systems have demonstrated remarkable accuracy, often boasting error margins smaller than a centimetre. The integration of machine learning has further elevated their reliability, allowing the systems to improve through experience and data accumulation.

Beyond mere correctness, automated line calling significantly enhances the pace of the game. Games can proceed without interruptions from disputes over line calls, maintaining momentum and player focus. This seamless operation is of particular importance in high-stakes tournaments where tensions run high and any delay can disrupt the psychological balance of the competitors.

Automated line calling also impacts the tenor of spectator experience. Fans now witness an added layer of drama, with the anticipation of a system validation becoming part of the match's theatre. As the virtual ball path plays on-screen, viewers are treated to a scientific display that substantiates the call, fostering greater engagement and understanding of the game's micro-moments.

The introduction of AI and automation into officiating practices prompts discussion around the evolving role of human judges. Although technology can capture indisputable data, the human element remains invaluable. Umpires stand as the ultimate arbitrators, interpreting data and maintaining the spirit of sportsmanship and respect on court. Essentially, automated systems serve as an aid rather than a replacement, assisting umpires in making lucid and fair decisions.

As with any technology, challenges persist. The implementation of automated line systems involves considerable costs, primarily affecting grassroots and amateur levels where budgets are tight. However, the progression of technology often translates to decreasing costs over time, promising broader accessibility in the future. Consequently, efforts are underway to develop more cost-effective solutions that leverage similar principles without the prohibitive expense.

Moreover, as AI continues to advance, we're likely to witness further sophistication in these systems. Future iterations may incorporate artificial intelligence that accounts for environmental factors like wind, speed, and player movement to enhance precision even further. As the technology evolves, the potential to introduce augmented reality features in training and player analytics surfaces, supplementing players' growth and performance strategies with intricate insights.

Incorporating automated line calling systems into tennis matches suggests a paradigm shift not just within tennis, but in sports at large, as similar technology gets adapted for other disciplines. The elegance with which such systems reconcile technology with tradition highlights their integral role in modernising the sport, ensuring that tennis remains a bastion of fairness and integrity.

In sum, while the spectacle of human-driven gameplay remains at the heart of tennis, automation and AI augment the calibre and fairness of the sport in ingenious ways. As we continue to explore the intersection of technology and physical prowess, the automated line calling system stands as a testament to what can be achieved when innovation respects and enhances tradition.

Court Management Systems

In the realm of tennis, innovation isn't confined to player performance or coaching strategies; it extends to the very environment where the sport is played. Court management systems are transforming the infrastructure of tennis, making it smarter and more efficient. These systems utilise artificial intelligence and IoT technologies to streamline court operations, enhance user experience, and optimise resource allocation. For a tech-savvy tennis community, these advancements unveil a future where technology and tradition harmonise on and off the court.

The implementation of AI-driven court management systems is revolutionising how tennis facilities operate. These systems allow facility managers to oversee court usage, bookings, and maintenance needs with unprecedented ease and accuracy. By integrating smart sensors and data analytics, court management systems can monitor and predict wear and tear, ensuring timely interventions and repairs. This proactive maintenance not only extends the lifespan of the court but also significantly reduces operational costs.

Automated booking systems are a cornerstone of modern court management. They facilitate efficient scheduling, allowing players to book courts online with minimal friction. These systems often come with user-friendly interfaces, making the booking process intuitive for players of all ages. Moreover, dynamic pricing algorithms can adjust court fees based on demand, ensuring optimal utilisation. This flexibility can lead to increased revenue, which can be reinvested into further improvements.

Additionally, AI-powered analytics play a crucial role in decision-making for court managers. By analysing data collected from various sources, these systems provide insights into player preferences, peak usage times, and overall customer satisfaction. Facilities can tailor their services to better meet expectations, whether by adjusting lighting for evening matches, ensuring cleanliness, or offering amenities that enhance the overall experience. This personalised approach can elevate a facility's reputation, attracting a loyal customer base.

The environmental impact of large facilities is another crucial consideration. Smart court management systems offer sustainable solutions, such as energy-efficient lighting and intelligent climate control systems. By adapting to real-time conditions, these technologies minimise energy wastage by illuminating only active courts or regulating temperature based on occupancy. In turn, facilities not only reduce their carbon footprint but also benefit from lowered utility expenses.

Security and access control within tennis venues have seen significant improvements thanks to advanced management systems. With smart locks and surveillance solutions, only authorised individuals can access courts and amenities. Facial recognition technology, card readers, or mobile apps can be employed to ensure seamless access while preventing unauthorised entry. This enhanced security fosters a safe and welcoming environment for players and staff alike.

Moreover, AI can significantly enhance guest experiences even before they arrive at the court. Predictive analytics can provide personalised recommendations for preferred times to play, suggest suitable opponents or doubles partners based on past match data, or even offer pre-match dietary advice. This level of personalisation transforms the tennis experience from merely recreational to a comprehensive lifestyle engagement.

For facilities with multiple courts or those hosting tournaments, efficient coordination is vital. AI-driven systems can handle the intricacies of scheduling multi-day events, ensuring proper allocation of courts and resources. They can automatically adjust for delays or weather disruptions, keeping matches running smoothly. This capability not only benefits players but also enhances organiser efficiency and spectator experience.

Beyond daily management, these systems can also support strategic planning. With comprehensive data reports and insights, facility operators can make informed decisions about expansions, marketing strategies, and investment in new technologies. By understanding usage trends and customer demographics, they can tailor offerings to target emerging markets or introduce new classes and programmes that align with community interests.

As tennis continues to evolve with AI, the role of court management systems becomes increasingly prominent. They represent a shift towards smarter, more responsive, and adaptable environments that align with modern players' expectations. Ultimately, these innovations allow for a seamless integration between the sport's rich history and its dynamic future.

It's essential to recognise that these advancements also broaden tennis's accessibility. As management becomes more efficient and costs are optimised, more individuals can enjoy the game, levelling the playing field and fostering a more inclusive community. The convergence of technology and tennis management holds the promise not only of enhanced athletic performance but also of a thriving sport that is ready to embrace everyone, springing from grassroots initiatives to professional showcases.

In conclusion, court management systems epitomise the transformation within smart courts and intelligent infrastructure. By harnessing AI's potential, they offer a blueprint for the future that accentuates both economic viability and environmental sustainability. As the sport of tennis undergoes this technological overhaul, its foundational elements of skill, passion, and community are poised to flourish, enriched by the very innovations driving change.

Chapter 6:
Wearables and Biometric Tracking

In the vibrant intersection of style and science, wearables are rapidly reshaping the tennis landscape with unparalleled precision. These sleek, unassuming devices not only collect vast swathes of biometric data but also deliver insights that redefine player performance and training regimens. Imagine being able to track heart rate variability, hydration levels, and muscle fatigue in real-time with just a flick of the wrist. This is not just about numbers but understanding the subtle dance between physiology and peak performance, making data-driven decisions seem almost innate. Coupled with sophisticated AI algorithms, wearables empower players and coaches to fine-tune their strategies, offering an intimate peek into how the body functions under pressure. The beauty lies in this seamless blend of technology and intuition; with every serve and volley, wearables ensure that athletes aren't just competing but are on a relentless quest for self-optimisation, making each game smarter and every player a pioneer in their own right.

Types of Wearable Devices

The evolution of wearable technology in tennis has not only revolutionised the way athletes approach their training regimen and matches, but it has also opened new doors to how the game itself is understood and analysed. As artificial intelligence continues its exponential growth, wearable devices have become indispensable tools for players and coaches alike, marrying technology with tradition in one of the oldest sports known to humankind. Each type of wearable brings something unique to the court, catering to a variety of needs and skill levels.

One of the most common types of wearable devices is the fitness tracker. These are often seen wrapped around a player's wrist, capturing a myriad of data points such as heart rate, calories burned, and steps taken. The magic lies in how this information is processed and interpreted. With advanced algorithms, a fitness tracker can provide insights into a player's cardiovascular endurance and recovery time. This is crucial for tennis players who must maintain peak physical performance across potentially gruelling matches that test stamina and resilience. The data gathered through these devices can shape daily workouts and recovery strategies, elevating a player's fitness regime to an entirely new level.

Smart clothing is another fascinating category making waves in the tennis world. Gone are the days when athletic apparel was merely about comfort and style. Now, embedded with sensors, smart shirts can monitor muscle activity and overall body movement. These garments provide real-time feedback about a player's form and biomechanics, allowing for immediate adjustments to enhance efficiency and prevent injury. This integration of technology and textile offers a seamless method of tracking performance metrics without burdening the athlete with additional gadgets, making it a preferred choice for those looking to keep things simple yet effective.

Next come the wearable cameras, often mounted discreetly on a player's cap or chest. While traditional video analysis remains popular, wearable cameras give a first-person perspective of the court, providing coaches and players with a unique vantage point that revisits plays and strategies from the athlete's point of view. This technology allows players to re-experience pivotal moments of a match, recognising areas for improvement or celebrating a well-executed strategy. Coupling this footage with AI-driven analysis can dramatically enhance strategic preparations for upcoming tournaments.

Smart socks and insoles are also introducing a new layer of sophistication in how footwork is understood and improved. These devices gather data about ground contact time, pressure distribution, and balance, which are critical factors in tennis where split-second movements can make or break a rally. By examining this data, trainers can design specific drills to improve agility and footwork, contributing directly to a player's on-court effectiveness.

Heart rate monitors stand as a testament to the age-old sporting mantra of knowing oneself. Though not exclusive to tennis, their application in the sport is profound. These monitors keep track of a player's heart rate variability, offering insights into their cardiovascular health and stress levels during high-intensity matches. Knowing how a player's heart performs under pressure can help tailor mental conditioning programs and ensure that an athlete's physical state is mirrored by their mental fortitude, creating a holistic approach to player development.

The more ambitious players and teams have begun deploying biometric shirts that do more than monitor muscle activity—they also track respiratory rates. Much of tennis is played at different altitude levels, where oxygen intake and breath control can be paramount to performance. By understanding how well a player is breathing during intense rallies, strategies can be adapted to maintain optimal oxygen flow to muscles, keeping fatigue at bay and focus sharp.

One cannot overlook the surge of popularity that virtual reality (VR) headsets are beginning to see. Though primarily used off-court, VR offers players an immersive environment to simulate matches, practice mental resilience, and replay specific opponent styles. It allows for mental rehearsal in a controlled setting, something akin to a mental workout that conditions players to think tactically under varying match scenarios. The insights derived from VR experiences enhance cognitive agility, marrying the mind with muscle memory to replicate real match conditions.

For the tech-savvy tennis professional, smartwatches offer a compact solution that combines many functions into one handy device. Beyond timekeeping, these watches sync with other wearables to offer comprehensive analytics on performance and fitness levels, delivering information to players and coaches easily and quickly. The convenience and functionality make them a firm favourite among those looking for an all-in-one wearable.

While wearable devices have diverse applications and benefits, it is crucial to understand that they are merely tools. The ultimate performance enhancement comes from how the information they provide is utilised. In a sport like tennis, where marginal gains can lead to significant competitive advantages, these gadgets guide athletes and coaches in making informed decisions about training methodologies and strategic approaches.

The future of wearables promises even greater innovation and integration with AI technologies. As devices become more embedded in athletic apparel and gear, their capacity to deliver precise and actionable insights will only increase. This seamless integration stands to transform biometric tracking into an intuitive experience that players hardly notice in their gear yet immensely benefit from in performance.

The fitness tracker for stamina tracking and recovery insight.

Smart clothing for real-time feedback on form and biomechanics.

Wearable cameras for first-person perspective and strategic revisit.

Smart socks and insoles for improving footwork precision.

Heart rate monitors for cardiovascular and stress analysis.

Biometric shirts for respiratory tracking and oxygen optimisation.

VR headsets for immersive match simulation and cognitive training.

Smartwatches for all-in-one data access and performance insights.

The integration of wearable technology and biometrics in tennis provides a comprehensive view of a player's performance, unlocking potential that's aligned with the vision of enhancing the sport through innovations. As we continue to embrace technology, the marriage of AI and human prowess promises an exciting horizon for tennis, propelling it into a future where success is measured not just by wins, but by the intelligence with which we play.

Data Collection and Analysis

In the rapidly evolving world of tennis, wearables and biometric tracking are quietly revolutionising the way data is collected and analysed. It's a marriage of technology and sport that brings unprecedented insights into player performance and potential. At the heart of this revolution is the sophisticated data these devices capture, ranging from heart rate and movement patterns to detailed biometric analyses.

Wearable devices such as smartwatches, fitness bands, and even smart clothing are becoming staples in a tennis player's toolkit. Their sensors provide real-time data, offering players and coaches a wealth of information previously untapped in the sport. This data isn't just numbers on a screen; it's a window into how a player's body responds to the stress and demands of a match. It can reveal insights that might take years to recognise through traditional means.

The process of data collection begins the moment a player steps on the court. Integrated sensors track every movement, capturing data points that include acceleration, speed, and directional changes. Advanced models even monitor muscle exertion and fatigue levels. This sophisticated level of tracking allows players to understand the nuances of their physical exertion and performance.

Biometric data comes into its own when combined with AI-driven analytics. Artificial intelligence scrutinises these vast amounts of data, drawing correlations and identifying patterns that might go unnoticed by the human eye. For instance, by analysing a player's heart rate variability and oxygen saturation during training sessions and matches, AI algorithms can predict the onset of fatigue and the risk of potential injuries.

Furthermore, players can now monitor how their bodies react under different conditions. Are they maintaining optimal hydration levels? How does altitude affect their performance? By analysing this data, players can make informed decisions about nutrition, hydration, and recovery strategies, all tailored to optimise performance on the court.

Coaches too are leveraging this data to craft more effective training regimens. The analytics derived from wearable technology provide a factual basis for developing personalised training programs. These tailored programs improve training efficiency by focusing on areas that need attention, whether it's enhancing endurance, speed, or agility.

Imagine a scenario where a player's training itinerary is dynamically adjusted based on real-time data insights. If the wearables indicate that a player is exhibiting signs of over-training, adjustments can be made on the fly, such as incorporating additional rest or modifying practice intensity. It's a proactive approach that not only enhances performance but also safeguards the athlete's health.

The implications of these advancements extend beyond individual training sessions. Match strategies can be refined and honed based on historical data and current physiological readings. Coaches can devise game plans that align with a player's physical readiness and opponent's weaknesses, all derived from the expansive datasets accumulated over time.

This data-centric approach also offers a significant competitive advantage in preparation and recovery. Customised recovery protocols, derived from biometric analysis, ensure that players are at their best when they step onto the court. Whether it's through tailored physical therapy or optimised nutrition, the insights gleaned from biometric data are pivotal in maintaining peak performance levels.

However, as with any technological advancement, there are challenges to be addressed. The integration of wearables and sophisticated analytics presents potential issues regarding data privacy and security. Protecting a player's data from misuse is paramount, ensuring that it's accessed and utilised responsibly to maintain fairness and integrity in the sport.

Moreover, the vast amounts of data gathered need to be distilled into actionable insights. The ability to interpret and leverage this information effectively is crucial. It's about transforming raw data into strategies that enhance an athlete's performance without overwhelming them or their coaches with too much information.

From a motivational standpoint, the insights received from data collection act as powerful drivers. Players gain an objective view of their progress, setting realistic goals based on their personalised data. For aspiring athletes, this technology provides a clear path to improvement, offering precise feedback on strengths and areas that require enhancement.

In conclusion, the fusion of wearables and biometric analysis with artificial intelligence is ushering in a new era of tennis. The data collected and analysed holds the key to unlocking a player's full potential, refining coaching methodologies, and shaping the future of training programs. As we continue to explore this frontier, the boundaries of what athletes can achieve on the court will undoubtedly be redefined.

Impact on Training and Performance

In today's hyperconnected world, where data is as prized as the gold of old, wearable technology has emerged as a game changer in the realm of sports. Biometric tracking offers detailed insight into athletes' performance, transforming how training and performance are understood in sports, especially tennis. As wearable technology continues to evolve, it's reshaping tennis training methods and player development, ushering in an era where precise, data-driven insights turbocharge athletes on their journey to excellence.

Wearable devices equipped with biometric sensors provide detailed real-time data across various physical and physiological parameters. This innovation has marked a significant pivot from intuition-based coaching to a more analytical and evidence-based approach. These gadgets can capture metrics from heart rate and calorie consumption to intricate movement patterns and even hydration levels. For tennis players, this means an unprecedented level of insight into their bodies and performance dynamics, empowering personalised training regimes that align closely with physiological needs.

Athletes benefit from such an advanced understanding of themselves because it translates directly into performance improvements. For instance, wearables can provide novice and advanced players with immediate feedback—everything from swing speed to footwork precision is monitored. The instantaneous nature of this feedback loop dramatically alters practice sessions' dynamics, making every hour on the court more productive than ever before. Coaches and players can recalibrate strategies on the fly, ensuring errors can be addressed and corrected promptly.

Moreover, the strategic implications of constant biometric surveillance are profound. With the ability to track how different training loads affect physiological metrics, athletes and coaches can better tailor training programs to improve performance while minimising injury risks. Over time, they can identify patterns and trends, ensuring training periods align with optimal performance windows. This efficient cycling between activity and recovery means athletes can push boundaries while remaining attuned to their limits.

From a psychological perspective, wearable tech fosters a unique dimension of self-awareness. Regular data insights allow athletes to identify their mental and physical states across different moments. For example, a player might notice stress indicators before critical matches or reduced heart rate variability during tournaments. Knowing this, they work with coaches to devise psychological strategies to help manage stress during high-stakes events, ultimately leading to a more composed player on the court.

Furthermore, training effectiveness isn't just about time spent on the court or in the gym but also about optimising recovery. Biometric tracking through wearables provides key insights into how athletes recover from both competitions and training sessions. Data pertaining to sleep quality, resting heart rate, and other recovery metrics can ensure players get adequate rest and rehabilitation, reducing the likelihood of overtraining, which is a common risk associated with traditional training methods.

Access to such granularity in performance data also democratises expertise in sports training. Historically, only elite athletes with significant financial and institutional backing could afford the cutting-edge analytics needed to elevate their game. With advances in wearable technology, more players across different competition levels can access comparable insights, thus levelling the playing field and potentially discovering hidden talents that might otherwise go unnoticed.

The collaborative nature of this technology also encourages new interactions within coaching teams. Seamless integration of data from wearables into training platforms means every stakeholder—coaches, nutritionists, psychologists—can contribute to a comprehensive development plan. A player's success becomes a project of collective effort, underpinned by data intelligence and collective expert input.

As data continues to flow from intertwining circuits to hands-on coaching discussions, ethical considerations around privacy and data protection invariably arise. It's critical to respect athletes' personal boundaries and ensure data is managed socially; transparent data-sharing agreements become as vital as secure data systems. Keeping athletes informed and in control of their biometrics goes hand-in-hand with the ethic of trust inherent in athletic coaching relationships.

The integration of wearables and biometric data is more than a technological advance; it's a cultural shift in tennis training philosophy. It doesn't just predict outcomes but influences the way athletes, trainers, and fans understand peak performance and the pathways to achieving it. As AI integrates these insights, we find ourselves standing on the precipice of a sports revolution where every stroke of genius on the court is backboned by streams of data that illuminate, inspire, and innovate the grand game of tennis. The future shines brightly for those who embrace this harmonious blend of tradition and technology, creating not just better athletes, but wiser ones.

The adoption of wearable tech in tennis is poised to become an intrinsic part of training regimens for years to come. As the technology continues to evolve and improve, further integrating AI, neural networks, and machine learning, the opportunities for refining these processes are boundless. The horizon is set for a future where the human body and mind, empowered by technology, push boundaries once seemingly unattainable, crafting a sports landscape as dynamic and vibrant as the athletes who inhabit it.

Chapter 7:
AI in Scouting and Recruitment

Imagine a world where finding the next tennis superstar isn't just a gamble but a strategic, data-driven process. AI has become a game-changer in scouting and recruitment, transforming how talent is identified and evaluated. Gone are the days when coaches relied solely on watching endless hours of footage and their intuition. Now, AI algorithms can sift through massive datasets, uncovering hidden gems with precision and efficiency. By analysing performance metrics, player biomechanics, and even psychological indicators, AI provides a comprehensive view, enhancing traditional scouting reports with an unparalleled depth of insight. This sophisticated approach allows recruiters to make more informed decisions, often discovering extraordinary talents who might otherwise have been overlooked. As a cornerstone of modern recruitment strategies, AI helps bridge the gap between potential and opportunity, ensuring that the future of tennis shines even brighter with a new wave of gifted players.

Identifying Talent with AI

In the evolving world of tennis, spotting young talent is as crucial as training current champions. Traditionally, scouting relied heavily on the keen eyes of seasoned scouts and coaches. However, the introduction of artificial intelligence is revolutionising this process by enabling more objective, data-driven assessments. AI not only helps identify potential stars but also mitigates human bias, ensuring that raw talent is not overlooked.

By using sophisticated algorithms, AI analyses vast datasets that include match statistics, training performance, and even biometric data. These metrics provide a comprehensive view of a player's capabilities and potential. Consider, for instance, the ability of AI to track intricate patterns in a player's movements. Such analysis can highlight physical agility, stamina, and precision in ways that were impossible a generation ago, opening new avenues for identifying talent even from the earliest stages of a player's development.

AI systems have begun to interpret video footage in a way that humans simply can't match in terms of speed and detail. By instantly analysing countless hours of play, AI can highlight players who excel in specific areas—be it serving, returning, or even mental resilience during high-pressure points. This capability helps talent scouts prioritise which players to monitor more closely, thus streamlining the entire recruitment process. Imagine being able to differentiate between a potentially great baseline player and an emerging volley expert just by reviewing AI-processed footage.

Moreover, AI tools are capable of historical comparisons, aligning the current form and stats of rising talents with benchmarks set by established players. This not only helps project potential career progressions but also aids in understanding how a young athlete's playing style may evolve. For instance, if a player exhibits serve efficiency akin to early data from a professional like Roger Federer or Serena Williams, scouts might take additional interest, aware of the traits that I might signal future greatness.

Beyond physical metrics, AI's ability to analyse psychological data is becoming increasingly valuable. Algorithms can assess a player's mental toughness—a critical component in professional tennis where matches can be marathons as much as sprints. By using data derived from biometric sensors, such as heart rate variability and stress responses, AI can predict how players might react under stress, offering insights into who may handle the pressure of high-stakes tournaments. This kind of analysis helps in identifying those players who might not only have the skills but also the temperament to reach the top.

The democratisation of talent identification, made possible by AI, ensures that prospects are discovered globally, not just in tennis's traditional strongholds. Local clubs and academies, previously limited by geographic and resource constraints, can now become talent hubs. By leveraging AI-enabled video and data analysis solutions, anyone from a small-town coach to a national federation can nurture talent with the same level of expertise once reserved for elite institutions.

AI's role extends into adjusting training regimens to focus on identified strengths and weaknesses, which in turn aligns with scouting requirements. For example, AI may uncover that a young player has exceptional natural agility but lacks consistency in their backhand. This data can inform targeted training to refine the player's techniques, enhancing their appeal to scouts and making them a more versatile asset on the court.

However, the rise of AI in talent identification carries its own set of challenges, particularly concerning ethical considerations and data privacy. As AI tools become more prevalent, ensuring the anonymity and safety of players' personal data must remain a priority. Agreements on how data is collected, stored, and used must be transparent, maintaining trust among players, parents, and the institutions involved.

The promise of AI in identifying talent also beckons a future where traditional and digital scouting methodologies converge. Coaches and AI systems are likely to work hand-in-hand, combining intuitive human judgment with objective machine analysis to form a holistic talent appraisal process. Such collaboration holds the potential to elevate scouting to new heights, ensuring that burgeoning talents are nurtured and guided effectively through their formative years.

With each passing tournament, AI's predictive accuracy improves, feeding on fresh, dynamic data to refine its talent-spotting abilities. For tennis, this means not only enhancing the current recruitment methods but assuring a future where even more diverse and well-rounded players emerge. By drawing on AI's capabilities, tennis stands ready to embrace an era where talent knows no bounds, breaking through geographical, economic, and cultural barriers. The stars of tomorrow may very well be shaped by today's algorithms, ushering in a transformative period for the sport.

Enhancing Scouting Reports

In the world of tennis, finding and nurturing new talent is paramount for maintaining the vibrancy and competitiveness of the sport. The rise of artificial intelligence (AI) is shaking up the traditional methods used in scouting and recruitment, offering a fresh, insightful perspective on player evaluation and potential. By integrating AI into scouting reports, tennis organisations can discern talent with a precision and depth previously unattainable.

Scouting reports have long served as the backbone for decision-makers in tennis recruitment. Traditionally, these reports relied heavily on subjective assessments from scouts, emphasising observations and predictions based on instinct. While subjective insight is invaluable, the limitation of relying purely on human observation is clear: it can be biased and lacks comprehensive data analysis. AI is changing this paradigm by offering data-driven insights that supplement the human eye and intuition.

AI can analyse an immense array of data points from match footage, including the velocity of serves, the precision of groundstrokes, and even the emotional responses of players during critical match moments. Through machine learning algorithms, it can identify patterns and tendencies that might elude even the most experienced scouts. This empowers teams and organisations to make informed decisions based on empirical evidence, enhancing the richness of scouting reports.

A vital aspect of enhancing scouting reports with AI lies in its ability to provide comparative analyses across a diverse pool of players. By aggregating data from various matches and tournaments, AI creates comprehensive profiles that compare each player's skill set, physical attributes, and mental acuity. This level of detail enables scouts and coaches to benchmark emerging players against established professionals, offering a clearer picture of the road ahead for up-and-coming talent.

The synergy between traditional scouting methods and AI technologies also plays a pivotal role in mitigating the risk associated with recruiting young players. Tennis, much like other sports, entails a high degree of unpredictability when it comes to the career trajectory of young prospects. AI tools can analyse biomechanical data, which gives insights into potential injury risks and longevity, helping organisations make prudent, long-term decisions.

Additionally, AI's integration into scouting allows for the exploration of untapped markets. Tennis has often highlighted prodigies who emerged from unlikely places, and AI enhances the identification of such talent by analysing performance metrics without cultural or geographical biases. By eliminating these barriers, the tennis community can discover promising players who might have otherwise gone unnoticed.

But it's not just about finding talent. AI-powered reports enhance developmental pathways by tailoring training regimes that address the unique needs of each player. Scouting reports generate a comprehensive plan that includes technical, tactical, and even psychological recommendations to help young athletes improve constantly. This personalised approach ensures that no stone is unturned in the quest for excellence.

Another transformative benefit is the timeframe within which scouting reports can be generated. Where human-only methods required extensive time for analysis and report generation, AI rapidly processes data to deliver almost real-time insights. This speed means scouts and coaches can spend more time implementing strategies rather than compiling them, ensuring they stay ahead in the competitive pursuit of new talent.

However, the integration of AI in scouting does come with its own set of challenges. It necessitates a shift in traditional mindsets, encouraging a more data-centric approach while ensuring that the human element of decision-making isn't lost. The challenge lies in balancing sophisticated analytical tools with the nuanced experience of seasoned scouts, ensuring both elements complement rather than compete with one another.

Trust in AI-generated insights is building, yet it is crucial to remain vigilant in interpreting these data-centric reports. Kolmogorov complexity or understanding the broad context of a player's performance is imperative. Thus, crafting well-rounded scouting reports demands collaboration between AI experts, data analysts, scouts, and coaches to create a holistic narrative around each player.

The continual evolution of AI technologies holds an even brighter future for scouting in tennis. As algorithms become more refined and the amount of available data grows, AI's ability to enhance scouting reports will only become more sophisticated. The prospect of AI predicting not just potential talent but also future performance scenarios is no longer a fantasy but a rapidly approaching reality.

In conclusion, AI-enhanced scouting reports signify a new dawn in tennis recruitment. As the toolkit available to scouts expands and becomes more precise, tennis organisations are poised to unearth talent in ways previously unimaginable. The marriage of technology and human insight ensures that the tennis world continues to evolve, driving the game forward while honouring its deep traditions and values.

Case Studies in Successful Recruitment

In the high-stakes world of tennis, uncovering hidden talent before anyone else can be a game-changer. Traditional methods of scouting have served well over the years, but now, the dawn of artificial intelligence is reshaping the recruitment landscape. Real-world examples illustrate how AI-driven scouting systems are not just supplementing traditional methods but are, in many ways, surpassing them. Let's explore some striking case studies that highlight successful recruitment through AI.

One of the most illuminating stories comes from a leading European tennis academy that integrated an AI-based platform designed for detecting emerging talents from an international pool of junior players. This system processed thousands of metrics, synthesising everything from match statistics to physical attributes, providing an analytical edge that human scouts couldn't consistently match. In a groundbreaking discovery, the platform identified a young player from Eastern Europe who wasn't even on the radar of most traditional scouts. Today, this player competes at the highest levels, owing much of his initial break to the data-driven insights of AI.

Another compelling case involves a national tennis federation that harnessed AI to revolutionize its junior selection process. Instead of relying solely on standard metrics like speed and technique, which are undoubtedly vital but often limit the big picture, the system analysed video footage using advanced computer vision algorithms. By assessing more nuanced elements—such as decision-making pace and the efficiency of movement across the court—the AI unearthed a promising talent who has since represented their country in international competitions.

The power of AI in scouting isn't confined to academies and federations. On the other side of the globe, a renowned tennis academy in the United States established a partnership with a tech firm specialising in AI-driven sports analytics. Their focus was on refining recruitment strategies by examining psychological metrics that predict perseverance and competitive spirit. AI-based assessments revealed cognitive and emotional strengths in players who otherwise appeared average through conventional scouting techniques. The result was the identification and nurturing of talent who, by the conventional wisdom, might have been overlooked.

Yet, these stories are not solely about the players found but about the transformative approaches AI enables. In Australia, a tennis club decided to implement an AI platform with a specific focus: diversifying their recruitment pool. This AI-driven model assessed not only players' current capabilities but also potential growth, forecasting the future stars among younger age groups who showed promise in other sports. This cross-sport analysis brought to light prospects with transferable skills—athletes who hadn't pursued tennis seriously but were encouraged to switch based on AI recommendations.

For college recruitment programs, AI has begun to redefine success parameters by fostering more intelligent engagements between potential recruits and coaching staff. Take for example a notable case from a collegiate tennis program in North America, which adopted an AI-driven platform for optimizing recruitment. Here, AI's role expanded beyond mere matching, suggesting tailor-made development programs for recruits to highlight both strengths and areas needing improvement. As a result, it wasn't just about launching a player's career, but ensuring their sustained development, and subsequently, boosting the college's success in league matches.

The narrative of talent discovery and AI doesn't stop at professional and semi-professional levels. Community-level clubs are now using simplified versions of AI platforms to identify local talent, thus providing opportunities that were historically limited to those having access to elite training resources. This democratization of talent identification not only fuels grassroots initiatives but ensures a continuously refreshed pool of players who might otherwise be sidelined due to resource constraints.

In examining these case studies, one might wonder what common threads stitch them together. It's the undeniable versatility of AI to handle vast data complexities and identify patterns invisible to the human eye. By assisting in unbiased evaluations, overcoming geographical limitations, and embracing a broader view of what constitutes potential, AI lays down a clearer path for talent to shine through.

As AI continues to innovate, sports organisations globally are poised at the precipice of a talent identification revolution. The lessons learned at these academies and clubs represent merely the beginning of how AI will infuse complexity and depth into recruitment strategies. The exciting part lies ahead, as AI becomes more adept, ensuring that the world of tennis never misses out on a star waiting to be found. What's crucial is recognising AI not as a competitor to human scouts but as an ally, augmenting their capabilities and sharpening the overall recruitment focus.

Chapter 8:
Enhancing Fan Engagement with AI

In the ever-evolving landscape of tennis, artificial intelligence serves as a dynamic force, transforming the way fans connect with the sport. Gone are the days when spectators merely watched from the sidelines. Today, interactive platforms backed by AI provide fans with unprecedented access to personalised content, tailoring the tennis experience to individual preferences. Augmented by virtual reality, supporters can now immerse themselves in matches as if they're courtside, witnessing the intensity and excitement first-hand. AI also plays a pivotal role in creating bespoke fan experiences, using advanced analytics to understand viewer behaviour and deliver content that resonates deeply. With these innovations, tennis isn't just a game to watch—it's an interactive arena where every fan can feel part of the action, enriching their connection to the sport they love.

Interactive Platforms

Interactive platforms are radically altering the landscape of tennis fan engagement, blending advanced technology with the intrinsic passion that fans have for the sport. At the heart of this transformation lies artificial intelligence (AI), which serves not only to enhance engagement but to create entirely new avenues of interaction between fans and the game they adore. Imagine a platform where fans can engage with matches in real time, not just as passive spectators but as active participants.

In recent years, AI has spearheaded the development of novel interactive experiences. Through smart algorithms and data analytics, these platforms are capable of delivering custom content. Whether it's a simulation of a player's shot selection or tracking the physical and mental dynamics during a match, these innovations allow fans to experience tennis beyond what's captured on the screen. It's more than just watching; it's immersing oneself in the game, gaining insights into strategies, and making predictions.

Engagement has been further amplified through platforms that incorporate virtual assistants and chatbots. These AI-driven assistants can answer questions, offer match statistics, or even provide historical context about tournaments and players. Imagine conversing with a tennis-savvy AI that can discuss match details or even provide a nuanced analysis of players on court. It bridges the gap between fandom and expertise, fostering a deeper understanding and appreciation of the complexities of tennis.

AI-driven chatbots add another layer of interactivity. They're versatile, handling everything from customer service inquiries for ticket sales to offering suggestions on where to find the best local tennis clubs. During major tournaments, these bots translate the high-level technical elements of the game into comprehensible information, essentially coaching the fans in real-time. Now, the armchair analyst or newbie to the sport can appreciate the intricate ballet of strategy and calculation unfolding on the court.

Moreover, interactive platforms powered by AI have reshaped the way highlights are presented to fans. Through advanced algorithms capable of detecting exciting moments like a killer serve or a breathtaking rally, these platforms automatically generate highlight reels tailored to individual preference. Fans with a penchant for epic comebacks or sensational volleys can curate their viewing experience, making the content uniquely personal and immersive.

The potential these platforms unlock is vast. Social media integration means that fans can share their custom-made highlights, initiate discussions, and even partake in live polls around match outcomes. It creates a thriving digital ecosystem where community engagement flourishes. The sense of camaraderie, traditionally found only in physical tennis clubs or during live events, has found a digital counterpart.

AI-fueled storytelling adds yet another layer. Platforms use AI to compile narratives around players' journeys, offering not just statistical data but also the dramatic arcs that punctuate their careers. Such storytelling does not merely dwell on victory and defeat but focuses on resilience, strategic evolution, and human triumph. It paints a complete picture of players as human beings, not just athletes. This narrative approach offers fans more context, enriching their emotional connection to the game.

Through adoption of such platforms, we observe tennis-fan interaction turning more personal and insightful. AI's ability to track user behaviour enables the personalisation of content, presenting enthusiasts with information they value. One could argue that these platforms provide the tools to craft their own tennis viewing and learning experience—something akin to an à la carte menu at a gourmet restaurant, providing exactly what whets their sporting appetite.

In parallel, integration with live interaction tools like augmented reality (AR) opens up unimaginable possibilities. Fans can simulate being court-side and engage with matches as if they were there, offering a multi-sensory experience without leaving the comfort of their home. The virtual space becomes a hive of activity where live stats are overlaid in real-time, and fans can even compete in predictive games, guessing plays or outcomes.

Despite the marvel that this technology brings, it raises discussions about the critical blending of digital and physical elements of tennis engagement. Enthusiasts ponder the line between enhancing experiences and detaching from the essence of the sport. The challenge, therefore, is to use these technological advancements to complement, not overshadow, the simple pleasure of watching a match unfold with all its raw emotions and unpredictability.

In conclusion, AI-powered interactive platforms are not just about augmenting interaction but democratising access to tennis in its full glory. It levels the playing field between the novice and the aficionado, making the sport more accessible and enjoyable. By transforming how fans experience tennis, these tools create a seamless blend of excitement and understanding. As AI continues to innovate, we can only anticipate how much further interactive platforms will go in redefining tennis engagement, ensuring that the passion for the sport only grows stronger.

Personalised Content

In today's digital playground, fans crave more than just watching a game on television—they yearn for an immersive, interactive, and personalised tennis experience. Enter artificial intelligence, transforming the tennis world not only for players and coaches but also for fans. With its formidable power to analyse mammoth datasets and predict user preferences, AI is revolutionising fan engagement by offering content that's finely tuned to individual tastes.

Imagine tuning into your favourite tennis match and, through AI-driven algorithms, receiving a customised viewing experience where highlights of your favourite players and unforgettable moments are in the spotlight. This capability grows from sophisticated AI systems capable of processing enormous volumes of data to pinpoint each viewer's preferences. From favourite player stats to the most thrilling match highlights, AI delivers content in a way that feels tailor-made. Understanding what captures a viewer's interest enables broadcasters and digital platforms to revolutionise the fan experience to unprecedented levels.

We'll see that, for the tennis enthusiast, personalisation isn't limited to video content. AI has extended its reach into tailored notifications, such as updates on tournaments involving your favourite players or alerts on emerging players to watch based on your historical interests. This embrace of AI fosters a stronger connection between fans and the sport, bridging distances and timelines to keep the excitement alive.

Another leap forward has been personalised analytics. Fans interested in diving deeper into match analysis can now access customised stats generated by AI—think player performance metrics or predictions on upcoming matchups. These insights are not just static numbers but dynamic, evolving with the season's progress and players' form changes. This caters to the analytically minded fans, offering an advanced understanding of the game and enhancing their viewing pleasure.

Social media has also been energised by AI's ability to deliver personalised content. Platforms utilise AI algorithms to curate feeds containing engaging content about tennis, from behind-the-scenes glimpses of players to trending discussions in the tennis community. This virtual engagement keeps fans connected, stimulated, and involved, offering an ongoing conversation around the sport that's engaging and meaningful.

Consider, too, the rise of virtual and augmented reality experiences powered by AI. While watching tennis matches through VR headsets, fans can choose their seat in the stadium, examining the match as if they were physically present. AI adds a layer of personalisation that adjusts the narrative and offers commentary based on known viewer preferences. In augmented reality, interactive overlays provide additional insights during live matches, including player stats or predictive shot trajectories, enhancing viewers' comprehension and enjoyment in real-time.

With these technologies, tennis becomes not just a sport to watch but an interactive spectacle where fans interact with the content on their terms. For instance, fantasy tennis leagues now harness AI engines to provide fans with players' performance analysis, suggesting strategic modifications to their fantasy teams. This creates a more engaging and competitive environment, encouraging fans to stay on top of player stats and rankings, ultimately enhancing their connection to tennis.

AI's role extends beyond merely altering the viewing and analytical experience. It plays a pivotal part in nurturing fan communities. By using AI-driven platforms to form communities based on shared interests, tennis fans can now connect globally, exchanging thoughts and experiences in real-time. These platforms utilise AI's linguistic capabilities to break down language barriers, creating a universally accessible environment.

The wealth of opportunities for personalising content in tennis points to an exciting future where engagement isn't just passive consumption but active participation. In this evolving landscape, the insights gathered from fans will further inform content creation, making the circle of personalisation even tighter. The more data AI absorbs about tennis fans' habits and preferences, the more precisely it can predict and tailor content offerings.

The technological advance in how fans engage with tennis is notable not just for its sophistication but also for the autonomy it offers to viewers in crafting how they experience the sport. The richness of this personalisation marks a transformative shift away from monolithic content models to ones that celebrate individual preferences. Furthermore, this progression isn't exclusive to the elite tennis fan with the latest gadgets; it increasingly permeates fan bases of all sizes and technology affinities.

AI's personalisation prowess suggests that the future of tennis engagement is poised to be even more interactive, enthralling, and inclusive. As technology continues to evolve, fans will enjoy ever more realistic, personalised, and meaningful interactions with the sport. Indeed, the possibilities are nearly boundless, promising a future where AI functions not just as a passive delivery mechanism but as an active, intelligent facilitator within the tennis experience.

As AI continues to break new ground in personalising engagement, it's remarkable how deeply these innovations resonate with the audience. Yet it's crucial to remember that the focus remains on maintaining the sport's essence and tradition—celebrating the talent, strategy, and thrill of tennis that has captivated fans for generations. AI doesn't replace these elements; rather, it enhances every part of the experience, making tennis more accessible and enjoyable than ever before.

In summation, the wedding of artificial intelligence with tennis allows fans to experience the game in ways previously only imagined. As AI learns and responds better over time, the level of personalisation will transcend current limitations, offering richer, more engaging content that satisfies the deepest interests and desires of every tennis aficionado. While technology unrolls its transformative capabilities, it also entices a profound connection between fans and their cherished sport.

Virtual Reality Experiences

As tennis evolves with artificial intelligence, a dynamic shift is occurring in how fans engage with the sport. One of the most exciting innovations is the introduction of virtual reality (VR) experiences.

These immersive technologies aim to bring fans closer than ever to the court, creating an environment where the thrill of the game can be accessed right from the comfort of their living rooms. The emergence and integration of VR into tennis are enhancing how people perceive and experience matches, making sporting encounters more interactive and exhilarating.

Imagine sitting courtside, the gentle thud of the ball against the racket palpable in each rally, the players' intensity almost tangible. This kind of presence, once reserved for a select few, is now within reach of any tech-savvy enthusiast with VR goggles. Artificial intelligence plays a crucial role in crafting these hyper-realistic scenarios, from reconstructing real-time physics of the game to developing lifelike environments that immerse fans in the essence of the match. The synergy between AI and VR is shaping a new frontier in sports engagement, one where the boundaries of reality stretch to meet our imaginations.

Virtual reality in tennis doesn't just replicate the traditional viewing experience; it revolutionises it. Advanced AI systems generate 3D environments tailored to individual preferences, offering customised perspectives and interactive elements. Fans can not only watch a match but also interact with it. They can choose their angle, decide which player to follow, and receive analytics in real-time, all integrated seamlessly into their viewing experience. It adds layers of information over the action, akin to an enriched reality that informs as it entertains.

To understand the impact of these experiences, consider the possibilities for fan outreach. Virtual reality transcends geographical barriers, allowing fans globally to feel part of events like Wimbledon or the US Open. AI-powered VR platforms enable people in different corners of the world to unite in their passion for tennis, breaking down physical limitations and creating a shared virtual space where the sport's community can flourish.

While live games hold a special place in the hearts of many, the accessibility of VR experiences is unrivalled. Events that may have been off limits financially or physically are accessible with a simple subscription. This democratisation of high-profile matches extends beyond viewing; it offers opportunities for fans to partake in virtual tournaments, practice sessions, or even VR-enabled coaching clinics. The virtual court becomes a versatile playground, blurring lines between spectator and participant.

The impact on the player's experience is just as significant. VR training modules, enabled by AI insights, provide athletes and coaches with a novel approach to strategy development. They can simulate different match conditions, challenges, and adversaries without stepping onto an actual court. Such advancements mean players can mentally and physically prepare for diverse scenarios, honing their skills in a controlled, virtual environment. This capability offers an edge that adapts effortlessly to the rigours of professional competition.

However, the potential reaches further than just adopting VR in live sports and training. The avenues for storytelling become unparalleled. VR can revisit historic matches, recreate iconic shots, or delve into underexplored angles of players' journeys, rendering them accessible in ways books or documentaries never could. Imagine walking with legends past, feeling the pulse of those significant wins or crucial losses, through experiences designed to educate and inspire.

Admittedly, as with any technological advancement, challenges accompany the introduction of VR into tennis. The intricacy of rendering high-quality environments in real-time demands robust hardware and cutting-edge AI algorithms. There's also the necessity to ensure VR systems are user-friendly, accessible across various devices, and compatible with existing tennis media platforms. These factors, while demanding, are met with eager innovation from tech companies striving to harness the potential of VR for tennis.

Future prospects for virtual reality experiences in tennis continue to expand, promising enhancements and novel features tailor-made for enthusiasts and professionals alike. AI-generated data can personalise these experiences further, gauging fan interest and tailoring content that matches their preferences. For instance, younger audiences may prefer interactive elements and gamified narratives, while seasoned fans might enjoy detailed analytic insights or historical match commentary.

As the line between physical and virtual engagement continues to blur, one can't help but reflect on the symbiotic relationship between tradition and technology. Tennis, with its rich history and grasped innovation, stands at an intriguing juncture. Virtual reality doesn't replace the sport's core essence but enriches it, ensuring the spirited dynamics of the court can be felt, understood, and appreciated on a broader, more inclusive scale. Whether experiencing the tension of a Grand Slam final or learning from a VR-coached drill, AI-driven VR ensures no fan remains too distant from the game they love.

In embracing these technological strides, tennis proves itself a sport capable of timeless appeal, adapted to the needs and whims of digital-centric enthusiasts. With virtual reality experiences at the forefront of fan engagement, tennis is not merely watched but lived.

Chapter 9:
The Role of AI in Injury Prevention

As we advance from previous explorations of AI's transformative impact on tennis, it's clear that its role in injury prevention represents nothing short of a revolution. With the integration of sophisticated predictive modelling and real-time health monitoring, AI is now a critical ally in safeguarding athletes' physical well-being, offering insights that were once unimaginable. It meticulously analyses vast amounts of biometric data to discern subtle patterns and indicators preceding potential injuries, thus enabling proactive rather than reactive measures. This ability to pre-emptively address issues equips players and coaches with strategies that could significantly elongate athletic careers. Moreover, AI's contribution doesn't stop at prediction; it extends to tailoring personalised rehabilitation and recovery programs, ensuring that players return to the court not merely healed but optimised for peak performance. Such advancements inspire a new frontier in athletic care, where AI not only aids in avoiding pitfalls but also in crafting a healthier, more sustainable athletic lifestyle.

Predictive Injury Modelling

In the high-stakes world of tennis, where milliseconds can determine the outcome of a match, the wellbeing of a player is of paramount importance. Enter predictive injury modelling, a solution where artificial intelligence intersects with sports medicine to minimise downtime and maximise player health. At its core, predictive injury modelling leverages vast amounts of data to anticipate injuries before they happen, turning potential setbacks into opportunities for enhanced performance and longevity in the sport.

The principle behind predictive injury modelling is deceptively straightforward: if we can understand the conditions that lead to an injury, we can intervene early and prevent it. Consider it akin to an early warning system that doesn't just sound an alarm but also suggests preventive actions. AI, with its capability to process millions of data points in the blink of an eye, is uniquely suited to this task. By analysing variables such as match intensity, training loads, biomechanics, and even psychological factors, AI can identify patterns that are invisible to the human eye but critical to predicting possible injuries.

This data-driven approach begins with the collection of real-time inputs from multiple sources. Wearable technology plays a crucial role here, tracking movements, physical exertion, and biometric data continuously. Each serve, sprint, and slide provides invaluable information. Combine this with health records and historical injury data, and you have a robust framework upon which predictive models can be constructed. These models, developed through machine learning techniques, enable customised injury forecasts tailored to each player's unique physiology and playing style.

Take, for instance, a player like Juan, who has a history of hamstring issues. Traditional approaches might rely on subjective measures, such as self-reported discomfort, to gauge when Juan should ease up. However, AI can provide a quantitative assessment, calculating the exact strain the muscle is under during various activities. Based on this analysis, a predictive model might suggest specific rest intervals or modifications to training regimens to mitigate risk, all while maintaining performance levels.

Coaches and physiotherapists are increasingly embracing this technological advancement, integrating AI insights into their daily routines. This doesn't mean the end of instinctive coaching, but rather a complement to it. The art of coaching is nuanced and deeply human; predictive injury modelling simply adds a new dimension—science-backed foresight. By identifying trends that precede an injury, coaches can develop strategies tailored to each player, balancing the demands of competition with injury prevention methods.

The benefits extend beyond just the player and coach. Tournament organisers and governing bodies also have a vested interest in ensuring their athletes are fit to compete. AI-driven injury models can inform scheduling decisions, optimising rest periods between matches to support player health over the long term. This kind of strategic planning can be essential for maintaining the enduring appeal of tournaments by ensuring that fans witness top athletes performing at their best.

Moreover, predictive injury modelling isn't solely for elite players. One of its most exciting aspects is its potential for wider application, spanning from junior players to veterans within the sport. By democratising access to these technologies, even grassroots programmes can benefit, introducing injury prevention strategies that keep young players in peak condition from their first serve. Just as we saw with computing and communication technologies, early adoption of predictive modelling can have a developmental impact that resonates throughout a player's career.

With rapid technological progress, predictive injury modelling is poised to become both broader and more precise. Advances in machine learning algorithms and data analytics hold the promise of integrating more complex datasets—from environmental conditions to genetic factors—sharpening predictions further. The future lies in creating an ecosystem where every player's health is continuously and holistically monitored, offering timely interventions that are both preventative and reactive.

Yet, as with all technological advances, it comes with its challenges. The ethical concerns surrounding data privacy cannot be overlooked. The accuracy of models hinges on the availability of personal health data, which requires stringent measures to secure this information. Balancing the need for comprehensive data with individual privacy rights is an ongoing dialogue, necessitating regulations and ethical guidelines to protect players' interests.

In summary, predictive injury modelling represents a frontier in sports science and medicine that is already redefining what is possible in tennis. By harnessing AI's power, the tennis community is not just reacting to injury but actively working to prevent it, nurturing healthier, longer, and more successful careers. Through collaboration between technologists, sports professionals, and governing bodies, the goal of reducing injuries is becoming an attainable reality, one data point—and one human decision—at a time.

Real-Time Health Monitoring

In the high-stakes arena of professional tennis, where the margin between victory and defeat can be razor-thin, maintaining optimal health is paramount. With the integration of artificial intelligence, real-time health monitoring has become a game changer, offering players and coaches invaluable insights they couldn't access before. Imagine a blend of technology that doesn't just observe but predicts and prescribes, allowing for interventions before issues escalate into injuries.

Today, AI-driven systems work seamlessly with wearables that track a range of biometric signals—heart rate, body temperature, and hydration levels, to name a few. These devices, often lightweight and unobtrusive, collect data at an astonishing rate, transforming it into actionable insights. Real-time health monitoring can alert a player to unseen stress levels, dehydration, or muscle fatigue while they're still on the court. This immediate feedback allows coaches to make crucial decisions regarding rest and recovery strategies in the heat of a match.

Through the lens of machine learning algorithms, patterns that could forewarn of injuries are identified with remarkable precision. For instance, by analysing movement patterns and fatigue levels, AI can predict the likelihood of developing stress-related injuries, such as tendonitis or strains. This stands in stark contrast to conventional systems where injuries are often detected well after they start to impair a player's performance. Now, players can be equipped with the knowledge to adjust their techniques or seek preventive treatments.

But real-time health monitoring isn't just about the avoidance of injuries; it's about optimising performance and longevity. AI assists in tailoring personalised health and fitness regimens that adjust dynamically based on ongoing data collection. The insights provided pave the way for bespoke training routines that keep athletes at the peak of their abilities without pushing them towards burnout.

The effectiveness of real-time health monitoring is magnified when data is pooled and compared against wider datasets from other players or even across different sports. This communal intelligence helps develop benchmarking metrics that individual performance can be measured against, identifying areas for improvement or necessary caution.

Moreover, mental health, often an overlooked aspect of an athlete's wellbeing, can be monitored in real time. AI models evaluate biometrics and behavioural patterns to assess stress levels and emotional states. Players who experience anxiety might find themselves more prone to mistakes. By understanding these cues, coaches can intervene with positive affirmations or strategic pauses, assisting players in maintaining their mental edge.

AI's role extends to remote monitoring, offering coaches and medical teams the ability to track an athlete's health from anywhere. This is especially beneficial during training periods spent at various international locations. A coach sitting half a world away can receive updates in real-time, ensuring continuity in training despite geographical divides.

Implementations of such technologies have shown tangible benefits. Not only are recovery times improved, but long-term health complications often associated with the rigors of professional tennis are mitigated. The enhanced longevity and sustained peak performance levels contribute to a more exciting and competitive sport.

The hurdles, however, aren't entirely absent. Ensuring data privacy and ethical usage of health data remains a continuous concern for governing bodies and technologists alike. Players must remain confident that their biometric data won't be misused, demanding robust security protocols and transparent data policies.

The influence of real-time health monitoring will undoubtedly escalate as AI technology becomes more nuanced and sophisticated. As sensors become more refined and less invasive, the ability to monitor and interpret health data will only improve. Players can expect an ever more intimate understanding of their physiology, potentially reaping benefits that extend beyond their tennis careers.

In essence, real-time health monitoring powered by AI isn't merely a tool for preventing injuries; it's an integral component of modern tennis strategy. This technology shapes the way players train and compete, fostering a more dynamic and safer environment in which to excel.

Rehabilitation and Recovery Programs

As tennis continues its evolution through the synergy with artificial intelligence, players' rehabilitation and recovery become a focal point of advanced technological innovation. It's no longer just about preventing injuries but facilitating faster, smarter recoveries when they do occur. The intersection of AI with injury recovery explores an intricate ballet between data analysis, personalised care, and cutting-edge technology.

Rehabilitation and recovery in tennis traditionally focused on physical therapy, rest, and monitored exercises, but AI has revolutionised this approach. Now, AI algorithms can analyse not just the mechanics of a serve or the arc of a shot but the subtle wear and tear on a player's body over time. By scrutinising data from wearables and court interactions, AI pinpoints stress points and suggests customised recovery programmes. This means personalising therapy to such a degree that it accounts for the athlete's unique biomechanics and injury history, helping prevent relapse and optimise return to play timelines.

One of the most significant capabilities lies in AI's ability to simulate various recovery scenarios. By leveraging predictive modelling, AI can trial and error different recovery strategies without the player having to endure them physically. This involves machine learning models trained on extensive datasets of athlete recovery patterns. With this technology, therapists and coaches can easily select the most effective rehabilitation regimen, reducing the time a player spends off the court.

Moreover, AI-driven rehabilitation tools offer real-time feedback. For instance, virtual coaches or avatars powered by AI guide players through prescribed exercises, ensuring the correct form and intensity. These virtual assistants adapt to the athlete's progress, ensuring each session is challenging yet attainable. This creates a continuous feedback loop that significantly enhances the effectiveness of recovery protocols.

AI's contribution isn't limited to the physical body. The mental aspect of recovery is paramount, and AI tools aim to support athletes psychologically during rehabilitation. Virtual reality (VR) environments, enhanced by AI, allow players to visualise themselves back in the game, maintaining a psychological edge. Virtual simulations that incorporate biofeedback aid players in managing stress and anxiety associated with injury, fortifying their mental resilience alongside physical healing.

While the technology is sophisticated, adoption requires a blend of human expertise and AI capability. Physiotherapists and sports scientists must interpret AI insights and translate them into practical strategies. AI doesn't replace the intuitive aspects of rehabilitation; instead, it augments professionals' capabilities, allowing them to base decisions on comprehensive datasets that were previously insurmountable to process manually. This synergy ensures that while the data is exhaustive, the implementation remains human-centric and tailored.

Remote monitoring systems further enhance recovery, offering players the ability to have their progress tracked without frequent visits to clinics. Athletes can perform designated exercises, record their efforts via wearable devices, and receive immediate evaluations. AI analyses this data in real-time, providing alerts for deviations that might indicate problems, such as fatigue or improper technique.

The role of AI in rehabilitation isn't confined to post-injury scenarios alone. In many ways, proactive rehabilitation—or prehabilitation—has gained prominence. By anticipating the biomechanical stresses of future games, AI can help craft recovery programs that preempt injuries. This forethought reduces downtime and helps maintain peak performance levels throughout the competitive season.

A concrete example of AI's transformative potential in rehabilitation is its application in tendon injuries. Tennis elbow, common among players, demands meticulous recovery protocols. AI systems now model the stress distribution across a player's arm during different strokes, tailoring rehab exercises that gradually rebuild strength without exacerbating the injury.

However, as with any technology, there are challenges. Integrating AI into rehabilitation programmes necessitates investment in both technology and training. For coaches and medical professionals who have spent years mastering traditional rehabilitation techniques, learning to trust and interpret AI output is a shift that comes with its steep learning curve. Nevertheless, the effectiveness of AI-driven programmes often outweighs the initial inertia, as evidenced by personalised player recovery times and improved long-term health outcomes.

As AI continues to gain traction, its integration within elite tennis training environments broadens. Institutions and professional clubs increasingly collaborate with tech companies to refine AI systems, urging a future where injury recovery is not just quick and effective but anticipatory and preventative. These partnerships hold the promise of creating robust frameworks for players at all levels, from grassroots to professional tiers.

Indeed, the future of AI-enhanced rehabilitation and recovery is promising. It holds not just a promise for shorter recovery periods but a vision of sustained player wellness and longevity in the sport. As AI systems grow more sophisticated, pulling insights from an ever-expanding pool of data, tennis athletes can look forward to a landscape where injuries no longer signal long absences from the game but opportunities to return stronger and more resilient.

Chapter 10: Optimising Coaching Strategies

In tennis, the art of coaching is undergoing a revolution thanks to artificial intelligence, which is transforming traditional strategies into sophisticated, data-driven tactics. Coaches now have unprecedented access to detailed analytics that allow them to tailor their methods to each player's unique strengths and weaknesses. Using AI, coaches can make informed decisions that enhance player performance, paving the way for personalised game plans and targeted skill development. Moreover, AI-powered tools facilitate more effective communication between coaches and players by providing actionable insights in real time. These innovations are not just optimizing strategies but redefining the entire coaching paradigm, setting new benchmarks for success. As a result, AI is becoming an invaluable ally in a coach's toolkit, fostering an environment where players are more engaged and better equipped to achieve their full potential. In this era of intelligent coaching, the boundaries of what can be achieved in tennis are continually expanding, offering thrilling possibilities for the future of the sport.

Data-Driven Decision Making

Within the modern realm of tennis, technology has become an integral partner in shaping strategies and enhancing performance. The rapid rise of data analytics has revolutionised how coaches comprehend and guide their players, bridging gaps that intuition alone might overlook.

In the landscape of tennis coaching, data-driven decision making stands out as a powerful tool, offering granular insights into every facet of the game.

Data-driven decision making empowers coaches to base their tactics not on gut feeling, but on hard evidence derived from extensive datasets. These datasets encompass everything from player performance metrics and match statistics to biometric data and environmental conditions. By analysing this information, coaches can devise more precise, effective strategies tailored to the unique attributes of each player.

At its core, data-driven decision making in tennis leverages the expansive capabilities of artificial intelligence to process vast amounts of information rapidly and accurately. AI algorithms can detect patterns in player behaviour, opponent strategies, and game dynamics that are beyond the scope of human analysis. With these insights, coaches can refine their approaches to maximise their players' strengths while minimizing weaknesses.

Consider a scenario where a player is preparing for a match against a particularly formidable opponent. Through data-driven analytics, coaches can scrutinise past encounters and identify patterns that might predict the rival's strategic preferences, shot selections, and weaknesses. Such insights enable them to craft game plans that exploit these potential vulnerabilities, giving their player a tangible competitive edge.

The role of data doesn't cease with pre-match preparations; it extends into live match situations as well. With real-time data streaming, coaches can adjust tactics on the fly during matches, responding dynamically to evolving conditions. This capability is crucial in a sport where the tempo can shift unexpectedly with just a few points. Data-driven insights provide a clearer understanding of when to push a player's aggressive stance or recalibrate to a more defensive strategy.

Moreover, data-driven decision making is not solely about tracking the competition. It also involves creating personalised developmental plans for each player. For instance, tracking long-term data can reveal areas of consistent improvement or stagnation, informing coaches on where to focus future training. These bespoke player profiles are invaluable in setting achievable goals, monitoring progress, and ultimately elevating performance sustainably.

It's interesting to note how machine learning models can dissect minute details, such as service patterns or stroke efficiencies, which may otherwise go unnoticed by the naked eye. By examining these elements, coaches can cultivate specific skill sets within players, optimise training sessions, and foster a holistic improvement in performance.

Equipped with these insights, coaches no longer operate based on conjecture. Instead, they provide feedback grounded in concrete evidence, leading to more meaningful discussions with players. This shift enhances the communication between coach and player, fostering a relationship rooted in understanding and trust. In this regard, data-driven decision making becomes a catalyst for psychological resilience and confidence, as players recognise that their strategies are underpinned by verifiable intelligence.

Still, the journey of adopting data-driven decision making isn't devoid of challenges. Integrating such an approach requires a paradigm shift in traditional coaching methodologies, demanding openness to technological innovation and continuous learning. Coaches need to be adept at interpreting data, which may necessitate collaborations with data scientists or analysts who understand the nuances of AI applications in sports.

Data-driven decision making also raises questions of data management and privacy. With an influx of data comes the duty of ensuring its ethical usage. Coaches must navigate these waters cautiously, safeguarding athletes' data while utilising its full potential to enhance performance.

Looking ahead, the role of data analytics in tennis coaching will likely expand further with advancements in AI technology. Future innovations might see even more sophisticated algorithms capable of offering insights with unparalleled precision, perhaps even predicting the outcomes of complex scenarios within the game.

In summary, data-driven decision making in tennis isn't just an enhancement—it's a transformation. It blends the artistry of tennis with the precision of science, weaving a narrative where empirical evidence guides the subtleties of human intuition and experience. Coaches who embrace this evolution in decision-making will not only gain a competitive edge but also cultivate a new culture of growth and adaptability in the tennis world.

Enhancing Communication with Players

Communication in tennis has always been pivotal, serving as the cornerstone of any successful coaching strategy. However, with the advent of artificial intelligence, this fundamental aspect of the sport is undergoing a transformation that is as exciting as it is revolutionary. The intricacies of communicating with players have been fundamentally altered by AI, bringing precision and personalised insights to the forefront of coaching.

In an age of data-driven coaching, the significance of clear, concise, and effective communication cannot be overstated. AI allows coaches to leverage technology to bridge gaps that were previously insurmountable. Visual tools powered by AI now enable coaches to break down complex data into understandable graphs and models.

This not only helps players to comprehend statistical analyses of their performances but also lets them see their strengths and weaknesses in real time, allowing for an interactive and engaging dialogue.

Consider a scenario where AI captures a player's movement and immediately translates it into feedback. Suddenly, abstract analytical concepts about footwork, swing speed, and shot angles become tangible. Players can interact with their own data on a screen, seeing what needs improvement and understanding why it matters. This visualisation is not just illuminating; it cultivates a deep connection between the player and the game strategy.

The traditional model of coaching often involved trial and error, with communication challenges being a prevalent issue—whether involving language barriers or simply the complexity in conveying technical nuances. AI has become a tool for clarity, allowing coaches to refine their communication strategies. Imagine AI act as a linguistic bridge, translating coach's insights into multiple languages seamlessly, thus addressing one of the oldest communication barriers in sports.

Additionally, AI introduces the concept of *adaptive coaching* where communication is tailored to suit the unique learning style and cognitive preferences of each player. By analysing behavioural patterns and past performances, AI can guide the coach in choosing the most effective communication strategies. Whether a player responds better to visual cues or verbal instructions, AI analytics assist in creating a customised communication protocol, making the entire coaching process more efficient and player-centred.

The role of AI extends beyond merely facilitating communication. It acts as a sentinel, tracking a player's physiological and psychological states. This monitoring becomes vital in knowing when to push a player harder or when to dial back and provide motivation instead of critique. Such insights foster an environment where players feel understood and valued, driving more open and productive conversations and enhancing mutual trust.

Such advancements have also opened up possibilities for remote coaching. Coaches can now interact with players from different parts of the world with real-time feedback and instructions. Video conferencing supplemented with AI analytics allows coaches to maintain effective communication channels without being physically present. This globalization of coaching strategies promotes a more inclusive approach to player development, giving promising players access to top-tier coaching irrespective of geographical barriers.

Moreover, AI isn't just refining how coaches communicate, but it's also equipping players to articulate their thoughts with higher precision. Players learn to interpret their own data, becoming more informed and engaged in tactical discussions. This not only makes them active participants in their own development but also fosters independent thinking and self-analysis, skills that are essential both on and off the court.

Despite these advancements, AI's role is to complement and enhance human communication, not replace it. The empathetic and motivational aspects inherent in human interaction continue to be a significant part of coaching. The nuances of a coach's tone, the supportive gestures, and motivational ethos can't be replicated by machines. AI supports the communication frameworks, but the art of coaching retains its human touch.

As AI continues to evolve, the potential to refine communication further seems boundless. Future advancements may include more sophisticated sentiment analysis tools that can detect emotional undercurrents in a player's speech and offer feedback on mental readiness. Moreover, AI might suggest the most opportune times for communication based on a player's mood profile, enhancing receptivity and effectiveness.

In essence, AI is the new theorist on the team, providing the data and logic, while the coaches remain the empathetic practitioners. Together, they create a triangulated communication strategy that balances analytics, technique, and human understanding, ultimately optimising the development path of players. This alliance promises a renaissance in how coaching strategies are crafted and executed, keeping the spirit of the sport dynamic while ensuring players evolve into their best selves both athletically and intellectually.

Integrating AI in Coaching Methodologies

The landscape of tennis coaching is being transformed, and we're standing on the brink of a seismic shift largely driven by artificial intelligence. As AI technologies continue to evolve, they're offering coaches an unprecedented toolkit with which to refine their methodologies and strategies. Where intuition and experience once ruled exclusively, now data and artificial intelligence are providing valuable insights that enhance traditional coaching methods. AI in tennis is not just a supplementary tool; it's becoming an indispensable ally.

Integrating AI into coaching methodologies doesn't mean replacing the human element. Rather, it's about augmenting a coach's innate understanding of the game with the powerful analytical capabilities provided by AI. This synergy allows for more precise techniques and strategies. For example, AI can analyse thousands of data points from a player's previous matches, offering insights into patterns and tendencies that might not be immediately apparent through human observation alone. This can include identifying a player's strengths and weaknesses, as well as those of their opponents, facilitating informed decisions on game strategy.

One of the critical ways AI aids coaches is through performance analytics. Coaches can dive into a plethora of metrics, from shot accuracy to energy expenditure, to ensure every aspect of a player's performance is optimised. By processing vast datasets, AI can forecast potential outcomes and provide strategic recommendations, allowing coaches to tailor their advice to each unique situation. This kind of detailed analysis supports strategic planning that can be fine-tuned to an individual player's style and strengths, something that was much harder to achieve before AI became involved.

Furthermore, AI-driven video analysis tools have redefined how coaches assess techniques and make corrections during training sessions. By examining high-definition footage frame by frame, these tools can detect even the subtlest errors in a player's technique. For instance, analysing the biomechanics of a player's serve or the footwork in alignment can yield insights that were not easily perceivable before, allowing for immediate and effective adjustments. Coaches are then empowered to offer more nuanced feedback, fostering deeper understanding and improvement in their players.

Despite the obvious advantages, integrating AI into tennis coaching poses its own set of challenges. One of the significant issues is the sheer volume of data produced. While it's true AI can sift through this data faster than any human, the skill lies in interpreting the results and translating them into actionable insights. Here, the coach's expertise still plays a critical role. AI may present the data, but it's the coach who contextualises it within the broader narrative of the player's development and goals.

Implementing AI technology in coaching also demands changes in infrastructure and mindset. Clubs and academies must be prepared to invest in the necessary software and hardware that facilitate AI analysis. Moreover, there's a learning curve as both coaches and players adapt to these new methods. The successful integration of AI into coaching methodologies, therefore, requires open-mindedness and a willingness to embrace new ways of thinking. Those who do can expect to gain a competitive advantage in maximising player performances.

As AI continues to underpin coaching methods, the relationship between coach and player is also evolving. Traditional coaching thrives on personal rapport and intuitive understanding. When AI insights enter the mix, it could initially seem impersonal. However, AI's role in data-driven decision-making only complements this relationship. Coaches can provide justification for their suggestions based on robust, objective data, which can enhance trust and communication with players. By being more informed, players are often more open to embracing change and pushing their boundaries.

Moreover, incorporating AI into practice sessions provides an avenue for personalised training that is both effective and efficient. Through AI, training routines can be customised to focus on areas needing improvement while reinforcing a player's natural strengths. For example, if AI detects that a player frequently struggles with backhand returns against specific opponent styles, training modules can be adjusted in real-time to concentrate on mitigating that weakness. Such specificity in regression and improvement efforts offers players a tailored path to success.

The potential for AI in refining coaching methodologies extends beyond player performance alone. It can redefine team dynamics and strategy. During doubles matches, AI can analyse player compatibility by examining various factors like individual playing styles, energy levels, and performance metrics. This analysis can guide coaches in forming partnerships that complement one another, considering not just the raw talent each player brings, but also how effectively they can interplay.

However, to truly harness the power of AI, tennis professionals—coaches and players alike—must collaborate with technology experts who can provide the needed technical knowledge and support. This interdisciplinary approach ensures that the integration of AI into coaching strategies not only becomes seamless but also stays at the cutting edge of innovation.

Artificial intelligence is dynamically reshaping the tennis coaching landscape, enhancing methodologies once governed by subjective judgement alone. In doing so, it's not about diminishing the role of the coach but empowering them with insights that were previously unimaginable. As AI becomes ingrained in coaching practices, the limitless potential of human-machine synergy beckons tennis towards a future where the sport is more strategic and compelling than ever before. For coaches ready to explore this new frontier, the journey promises to be as rewarding as it is revolutionary.

Chapter 11:
AI-Driven Mental Conditioning

The burgeoning role of artificial intelligence in tennis is not only transforming the physical aspects of the game but also revolutionising mental conditioning. Today, AI tools are meticulously analysing psychological metrics, offering athletes and coaches insights into the cognitive and emotional domains that were once elusive. This AI-driven approach empowers players to manage stress more effectively, enhancing their mental resilience through tailored strategies that account for individual psychological profiles. With AI, the path to mastering one's mental game is paved with precision and personalisation. Advanced stress management tools, underpinned by AI, provide real-time feedback and adjustment, enabling players to maintain composure even under the most intense court pressure. By integrating AI in mental training programs, athletes are not just honing their skill sets but also shaping their mental fortitude, leading to remarkable performances and longevity in their careers. Through case studies of successful implementations, the profound impact of AI on mental conditioning reveals itself, offering a glimpse into a future where technology and psychology converge to foster not only agile athletes but also unyielding minds.

Psychological Metrics

In the evolving landscape of tennis, where technology entwines with the human element, understanding psychological metrics is becoming indispensable. As the game has progressed from intuition-led strategies to data-driven tactics, so has the emphasis on mental resilience and psychological insights. In this context, AI plays a transformative role. Operating beyond traditional metrics, AI now enables coaches and players to delve into the psychological side of training and competition, providing a window into new dimensions of athlete well-being and performance.

One of the primary applications of AI in processing psychological metrics is in tracking and analysing stress levels. Tennis is undoubtedly a mentally taxing sport. Players contend not just with their physical opponents but also with internal pressures and psychological battles. Here, AI-driven systems monitor physiological responses—such as heart rates and cortical activity—to infer stress levels. This analysis is vital in developing effective stress management strategies, ultimately boosting a player's ability to handle high-pressure situations.

AI systems can offer invaluable insights through real-time feedback. By tracking a player's heart rate, sweat levels, and breathing patterns, these systems can infer psychological states like anxiety or focus levels and allow for instantaneous adjustments. During training sessions, this data helps players and coaches identify stress triggers and explore techniques to regain composure and maintain optimal performance. Hence, AI becomes a silent, yet effective partner, allowing athletes to achieve a heightened state of self-awareness.

The application of AI also extends into motivational metrics, examining a player's intrinsic motivation levels. Through sentiment analysis and AI-enhanced questionnaires, players can outline their mental states and motivational barriers. The data collected enhances personalisation, allowing coaches to adapt motivational techniques that speak to individual athletes' needs rather than relying on generic, one-size-fits-all solutions.

Furthermore, AI actively contributes to the advancement of emotional intelligence in tennis players. It does so by analysing players' interactions, language, and expressions during matches and training. Such analysis opens doors to understanding emotional patterns and improving players' communication and relationship-building skills. This is especially critical in doubles matches, where synergy and mutual understanding between partners can greatly influence performance.

Besides improving mental and emotional awareness, AI cultivates resilience, aiding players in bouncing back from setbacks. By analysing historical data of past performances and psychological responses to victories and defeats, tailored training programs can be developed to fortify mental toughness. Players become more adept at processing losses constructively, turning them into learning opportunities that fuel future success.

The integration of AI into psychological training also fosters the development of visualisation techniques, which are essential for peak performance. Players can immerse themselves in simulated scenarios that mirror match-day conditions, guided by AI cues and feedback. Such simulations not only enhance strategic planning but also condition the mind to remain steady and focused amidst the cacophony of real-world distractions.

The role of AI in the realm of psychology also influences team dynamics and leadership skills. Through AI-driven insights, both players and coaches are better positioned to cultivate an atmosphere of trust and cohesion. Since leadership in sports often requires a deep understanding of team members' psychological states, AI provides the necessary tools to comprehend and respond to the fluctuating dynamics within a team.

In essence, AI acts as a bridge between the tangible and intangible aspects of sport, seamlessly connecting physiology, performance, and psychology. By employing psychological metrics, AI allows coaches and sports psychologists to go beyond traditional training paradigms, shaping comprehensive mental conditioning strategies. The ability to synthesise cognitive and emotional data translates into a competitive psychological edge that empowers players not only to excel on the court but also to nurture a healthier mindset off it.

As AI continues to expand its footprint in tennis, its role in psychological conditioning becomes increasingly pivotal. By deepening our understanding of these metrics, coaches and players can harness AI's full potential, evolving not just as better competitors, but as individuals equipped to handle the multifaceted challenges of modern sports. The path forward invites an ongoing dialogue between technology and human intuition as we refine the art of tennis through the lens of AI.

Stress Management Tools

In the high-stakes world of tennis, stress is as constant as the bouncing of a ball. Off the court, however, artificial intelligence is actively developing innovative methods to ease this omnipresent pressure. Stress management tools powered by AI are emerging as an invaluable asset for both players and coaches, helping to enhance mental resilience by offering bespoke strategies tailored to an individual's psychological profile. By leveraging data, these tools provide insights that previously required a team of psychologists or were left largely to intuition.

At the core of these AI-driven stress management tools is the ability to comprehend and analyse vast amounts of data from various sources. This data is not limited to match performances but also includes physiological and emotional metrics that players generate on and off the court. For instance, wearables track heart rate variability, a crucial indicator of stress levels, to forecast when a player's stress may become detrimental to their performance. Such predictive capabilities allow for timely interventions, ensuring athletes remain at their mental best.

AI's prowess in pattern recognition is another significant advantage. By analysing historical data about a player's performances in different stress-inducing situations, AI can identify triggers and patterns that lead to stress. This enables the crafting of individualised strategies that focus on mitigating these triggers, whether it's a particular match situation, a specific opponent, or even environmental conditions. Such analyses equip coaches and players with the foresight needed to approach games with a more relaxed, yet focused, mindset.

Beyond mere analysis, AI-driven applications have taken stress management a step further by offering interactive solutions. Apps utilising machine learning algorithms can learn from a player's feedback, adjusting and tailoring coping strategies in real time. Through gamification, these apps can make stress management more engaging, encouraging players to practice mindfulness exercises or engage in quick mental health checks that keep stress levels in check without adding additional burdens.

Furthermore, virtual reality (VR) integrated with AI offers a revolutionary approach to stress management. Players can simulate stressful match scenarios in a controlled, virtual environment, allowing them to practice stress-reducing techniques in situ. This technology provides a safe space to confront and adapt to stressful conditions without the real-world consequences of a poor performance, thus gradually building a player's stress resilience.

Coaches, too, benefit indirectly from AI stress management tools. As they gather insights about their players through these tools, they can tailor training sessions not just to address physical skills, but to incorporate mental conditioning. This approach fosters a more holistic preparation strategy, where mental wellbeing is considered just as crucial as physical fitness. It revolutionises coaching by seamlessly integrating psychological readiness into traditional sports strategies.

The advantages of AI in stress management for tennis don't stop with individual players or coaches. On a broader scale, these innovations contribute to the overall improvement of mental health support across the sport. As AI gathers more data from diverse players, it creates a more comprehensive understanding of common stress triggers and coping mechanisms. This, in turn, fuels further innovation and more sophisticated tools, which can be adapted to different player archetypes or even to other sports.

However, the integration of AI-driven stress management tools also presents new challenges. There are data privacy concerns and the need for ethical considerations in how sensitive information is handled. Maintaining a player's trust requires transparency and strong safeguards around data use. The ease with which AI can process personal data means that practitioners in tennis must strike a delicate balance between technological effectiveness and ethical responsibility.

Moreover, while AI provides unparalleled insights and assistance, it is not a panacea for all stress-related issues. At times, the human touch remains irreplaceable. Players benefit from one-on-one interactions with coaches and psychologists who can provide empathetic support that AI cannot yet emulate fully. It's crucial to view AI as a complement to traditional methods rather than a replacement. Successful integration involves a symbiotic relationship where AI and human expertise work hand-in-hand.

As tennis continues to evolve with technological advancements, AI-driven stress management tools will likely become even more prevalent and sophisticated. The ongoing refinement of these technologies promises to provide deeper insights and more effective strategies. The future may hold AI applications capable of not only identifying stress but also prompting proactive behavioural adjustments, predicting stress impacts on match outcomes, and offering dynamic, situation-specific guidance.

In summary, AI's role in stress management in tennis is an exciting development that offers comprehensive and customisable solutions to one of the sport's most enduring challenges. It addresses immediate stress factors while setting new standards for mental conditioning. The fusion of cutting-edge technology with human intuition is setting the stage for a new era where mental fortitude can be reinforced just as robustly as physical prowess, ultimately enhancing the competitive spirit of tennis in unprecedented ways.

Case Studies in Mental Resilience

Mental resilience stands as a cornerstone of success in tennis, where the pressure of competition can erode even the most talented players' performances. AI-driven mental conditioning has begun to revolutionise how players approach this aspect of the game. By leveraging vast data and cutting-edge algorithms, AI offers innovative tools for developing mental fortitude, built not only from traditional psychological insights but from patterns unearthed in vast data sets.

One illustrious case study involves a top-ranked female tennis player who struggled with maintaining composure during high-stakes matches. Her team integrated AI-based stress management tools, which utilised heart rate variability data and feedback from wearable devices to create personalised meditation and breathing exercises. These exercises were tailored to the player's unique physiological responses under pressure. Over time, as real-time data continued to inform the refinement of these techniques, she noted not just an improvement in her emotional regulation but a significant boost in her confidence levels during crucial points.

AI's role was not confined to merely offering relaxation techniques. It also extended to understanding the athlete's mental triggers. A renowned tennis academy use AI algorithms to analyse player interviews, game footage, and biometric data. The system identified specific behaviours and postures indicative of peak stress levels and unearthed patterns leading up to these moments. Armed with this AI-generated insight, coaches could offer precise interventions. Players learned to recognise and manage these stress indicators, transforming potential weaknesses into opportunities for growth.

In a different scenario, a promising young player on the cusp of breaking into the professional circuit faced challenges with overthinking. Her analytical mind often detracted from her instinctual play. AI-driven analytics pointed to this pattern through a series of scrimmages, suggesting a mental bottleneck that repeatedly cropped up during competitive play. By pairing AI-derived insights with cognitive behavioural approaches, her team developed a strategy that enhanced her instinctive decision-making. She re-learned how to trust her gut, resulting in more fluid and intuitive matches, catapulting her upwards in the rankings.

These case studies indicate how AI doesn't just support players by managing stress and anxiety: it redefines the mental game. For a mid-ranking player, battling with inconsistency, an AI system focused on psychological metrics helped decode complex emotions tied to on-court performance. By collecting data across numerous matches, AI revealed that certain stress responses were in fact beneficial — they aligned with peak performance events. Coaches used these insights to teach the player how to channel these responses positively, turning perceived pressure into a performance lever.

A shared characteristic across these studies is the tailored aspect of AI systems. Unlike traditional psychological methods that follow generalised principles, AI allows customisation to the nth degree. This personalisation is particularly crucial in a sport like tennis, where the individual nature of competition means that each player's psychological needs can vary dramatically. AI's ability to adapt and iterate quickly renders it a powerful tool for mental conditioning, offering insights that standard psychological tests might overlook.

Moreover, these adaptations aren't limited to professional realms. Junior players benefit tremendously from AI-driven mental conditioning too. Young tennis players often face unique challenges related to pressure, expectations, and identity at a formative stage. AI-driven applications use gamified frameworks to engage these budding athletes, providing cognitive exercises that subtly enhance their mental resilience without the overt intensity of professional sports psychology. Such applications not only prepare young players for future competitive environments but also offer life skills in stress management.

AI-driven mental conditioning also holds promise in team dynamics, prevalent in doubles or tennis camps. AI analytics, equipped with advanced sentiment analysis, can gauge team cohesion and individual emotional states. Successful teams often attribute their wins to strong interpersonal dynamics, a factor AI can optimise by identifying tension points and fostering better communication. As doubles teams learn to synchronise their strategies with AI assistance, they harness collective mental strength, often a game-changing advantage in clutch moments.

Notably, mental resilience isn't just about managing stress or anxiety; it's about a comprehensive approach to mental fortitude, incorporating focus, motivation, and the ability to rebound from setbacks. AI-driven training modules now include virtual reality scenarios that recreate match situations. Players train under artificially induced stress conditions, honing cognitive resilience in simulated environments that mimic live-game pressure.

The overarching takeaway from these studies is the potential for AI to fundamentally reshape how we understand mental resilience in tennis. By marrying psychology with technology, AI-driven mental conditioning becomes a dual-edge sword, sharpening the mind while liberating it from the shackles of traditional sports psychology limitations. As AI systems become more advanced, their contributions to player mental resilience promise a future where athletes are not just physically honed but mentally invincible, ready for the unpredictable nature of competitive tennis.

Chapter 12:
The Future of Tennis Analytics

As we stand on the cusp of a new era in tennis, the incorporation of AI-driven analytics promises to propel the sport into an unprecedented realm of precision and insight. Emerging technologies promise enhanced player performance analysis, bringing clarity to intricate patterns that were once the domain of intuition alone. With real-time data processing evolving at a breakneck pace, the capability to forecast trends and anticipate outcomes will become increasingly refined. These innovations could revolutionise both on-court strategies and off-court training methodologies. Enthusiasts, coaches, and players alike are on the brink of accessing intelligent systems that not only observe player motions but also delve deeper into the psychology of play and the nuanced strategies that differentiate victory from defeat. Such advancements will likely redefine how we understand and experience tennis, creating a future where analytics not only inform but inspire the game. As these technologies find their footing, they offer a staggering glance into what lies ahead—a future where the synergy between human skill and digital enhancement creates a playing field ripe with unbounded potential.

Emerging Technologies

The world of tennis is on the cusp of a technological revolution, driven primarily by the integration of emerging technologies that are setting new benchmarks in analytics. Unlike the familiar tools that gradually evolved over years, these innovations promise to reshape the game fundamentally and rapidly. From algorithms analysing every stroke to devices predicting player fatigue, the landscape of tennis is becoming both intricate and exhilarating.

Let's consider quantum computing. While it may sound like science fiction, this cutting-edge technology is steadily making its way into sports analytics. Quantum computers, with their unmatched processing power, have the potential to handle complex datasets at speeds far beyond current capabilities. This means they could conduct real-time analysis of a player's performance, incorporating thousands of data points previously deemed too intricate for traditional systems. Imagine being able to analyse not just the trajectory of every ball but also the micro-adjustments a player makes subconsciously during intense rallies.

Another game-changer is augmented reality (AR). While we all enjoy the experience of watching the game on a screen, AR is set to immerse us further, transforming our perception of the sport. Picture this: coaches and players donning AR glasses on the court, receiving instant visual feedback on ball trajectories, optimal shot placements, and even opponent weaknesses. This tech arms them with insights that are not only instant but incredibly detailed, offering an innovative edge in training and competitive environments.

Artificial intelligence (AI) is already playing a pivotal role, yet its future in tennis promises even more. Imagine AI systems that anticipate not just the outcome of a match but predict strategies several games ahead. Such systems are being developed to learn player behaviour, strategy effectiveness, and even the psychological state of athletes. They forecast trends by building models that assimilate historical data, on-court performances, and personal player psychology. This goes far beyond mere match statistics, delving into a realm of predictive analytics which offers unprecedented insights.

The integration of the Internet of Things (IoT) in tennis infrastructure signifies another monumental shift. Smart courts are now a familiar concept, but innovations in IoT are enhancing their capabilities significantly. IoT can create a networked ecosystem on the court where rackets, balls, player attire, and even court surfaces communicate seamlessly. It enables the collection of a vast array of metrics in real-time, from racket speed to foot pressure distribution, helping players and coaches gain a deeper understanding of performance nuances with remarkable precision.

On the horizon is the exciting potential of neuromorphic computing, inspired by human neurobiology. Unlike traditional computers, neuromorphic systems can process massive amounts of sensory data in a similar way to the human brain. This ability could eventually translate to real-time shot decision-making aids for players, helping them refine split-second choices during high-stakes matches. It also opens avenues for mental training applications, providing an in-depth understanding of cognitive processes under competitive stress.

Then there are blockchain technologies, whose impact, though indirect, could be profound. Secure data sharing among players, coaches, and analysts can transform how analytics are utilised. By recording all data transactions immutably, blockchain could safeguard player metrics, ensuring data integrity and boosting trust in analytic outcomes. This fosters an environment where players feel more secure sharing their performance data, potentially leading to a boon in collaborative data analysis and learning.

Incorporating these emerging techs doesn't just refine tennis analytics; it fundamentally changes player experiences and training methodologies. Coaches can customise development programs with greater effectiveness, tailoring every training session to address minute deficiencies or nurture specific skills based on solid data rather than intuition or experience alone.

While all these technologies are exciting, they bring about challenges that need addressing. Ensuring seamless tech integration without disrupting the game's flow is imperative. The balance between maintaining the sport's traditional appeal while embracing a technology-driven future will be delicate but crucial. Additionally, players' concerns over privacy and the ethical use of data must be handled adeptly to keep the spirit of the game intact.

Therefore, as we look ahead, it's vital to remain adaptable and open-minded. Tennis, at its core, remains a beautiful symphony of skill and strategy, and with emerging technologies, it's bound to become even more finely orchestrated. By embracing these advancements thoughtfully, the sport can evolve in ways that enhance authenticity while simultaneously meeting the demands of a tech-savvy and performance-driven future.

In essence, the emerging technologies in tennis analytics are not just about statistics or performance metrics. They represent a paradigm shift – a future where decisions on and off the court are backed by an unrivalled level of intelligence and insight. With the right blend of innovation and tradition, the future of tennis is an open court for technology to play its best game. The possibilities are limitless, and the implications are as promising as they are profound.

Forecasting Trends

As the landscape of tennis continuously evolves with the introduction of advanced technologies, forecasting trends in tennis analytics reveals not only the potential developments on the horizon but also the revolution pending for both athletes and enthusiasts alike. Through the complexities of artificial intelligence, new opportunities are emerging that promise to redefine how we perceive, analyse, and experience tennis. These trends highlight pathways where data-driven insights and machine learning will compel the sport into an era of heightened competitiveness and engagement.

When considering the future trajectory of tennis analytics, several emerging technologies stand out. One such innovation is the growing application of computer vision in video analysis. This technology, capable of tracking player movements and ball trajectories with incredible precision, allows for a deeper insight than ever before. The implications for training sessions are vast. Coaches can leverage these insights to tailor training programmes to individual needs, while players can focus on refining techniques in a manner that's never been possible—enhancing precision down to the millisecond.

The potential of wearable technology will also see a surge in the coming years. As these devices become more sophisticated, they will provide real-time feedback on various biometric data points, including heart rate variability, muscle fatigue, and hydration levels. This information equips players with the ability to adjust on the fly, optimising performance during both training and live matches. Additionally, combining this information with AI-driven software can yield predictive analysis, offering forecasts on potential injuries, performance dips, or even strategic advantages based on past behaviours.

Data is undoubtedly at the heart of these advancements. Machine learning algorithms continue to evolve, transforming mountains of seemingly disparate data into actionable intelligence. In the future, tennis analytics will likely harness these capabilities to offer dynamic coaching strategies that adapt mid-match, providing tactical adjustments that respond to an opponent's weaknesses or exploiting emerging opportunities as they arise. This level of real-time assessment and adjustment opens avenues for creating matches that are not only competitive but also unpredictable, enhancing the spectacle for fans.

Developments in collaborative AI further complement this data-centric approach. Imagine a comprehensive AI system capable of conversing and collaborating with coaches and players alike, providing consultation on strategies and offering innovative solutions informed by multitudes of match data. This evolving trend could transform the role of traditional coaching, making it more integrated and interdependent with technology than ever before.

Fan engagement platforms are not to be left behind in this transformation. With AI, personalised content delivery is set to become the norm, where data on viewing habits and preferences shapes the tennis experience of each fan. From selecting the highlights of matches based on individual interests to offering interactive elements during live games, AI's capacity to enhance the spectator experience is almost limitless. Such systems are anticipated to bring fans closer to the action, creating a more intimate and interactive viewing experience that caters to a global audience.

There's also a shift in how tennis tournaments might operate in the coming years. Leveraging AI to predict outcomes and optimise logistics could streamline the setup and execution of multi-national events. AI algorithms might be employed to predict weather conditions, player availability, or even audience preferences, making global tournaments not just more efficient but equally inclusive and diverse in their offerings.

The sporting body's governance and regulatory frameworks will also have to adapt to accommodate these burgeoning technologies. As AI continues to ingrain itself deeper into the sport, policies ensuring fair and ethical usage will be vital. The trend here suggests a balanced approach where innovation is fostered while maintaining the integrity and spirit of tennis.

However, the role of AI is not constrained only to professional realms. Tennis at the grassroots level stands to benefit significantly from these trends. AI-driven analytical tools could be accessible even for amateur players, democratising high-level coaching insights and allowing talent from all walks of life to emerge. By enabling a broader access to previously elite-level insights, AI fosters an inclusive environment—bridging the gap between aspiring juniors and seasoned professionals.

Lastly, as the narrative unfolds, the question arises: How will these trends coalesce to forge new pathways in tennis analytics? The answer lies in the symbiotic relationship that AI will ultimately establish with the human elements of tennis. By fostering adaptability and learning within each sector of the sport, AI will not replace the invaluable human insight; instead, it will enhance it and elevate the sport of tennis to extraordinary new heights. The future beckons a partnership between technology and tradition, paving the way for unprecedented growth and a renewed sense of connectivity within the tennis community.

Potential Innovations

The fusion of cutting-edge technology with the traditions of tennis has opened a new realm of possibilities that were once confined to the imaginations of science fiction writers. The potential innovations in tennis analytics are set to redefine how players, coaches, and fans experience the sport. With the continual advancements in artificial intelligence, we can look forward to more deeply integrated systems that will provide unparalleled insights into every aspect of the game, paving the way for innovations that will enhance performance, ensure fair play, and personalize the viewer experience like never before.

One of the most exciting areas of innovation lies in the realm of real-time data processing. Future systems could potentially analyze matches live, offering instant feedback on player performance and strategy. Imagine an AI capable of not only identifying weaknesses in an opponent's game but also suggesting strategic adjustments mid-match. This kind of real-time analysis could revolutionize coaching, allowing trainers to tweak game plans instantaneously and with pinpoint accuracy, enabling players to adapt dynamically to the evolving nature of each match.

Virtual and augmented realities are other fields ripe for development in tennis. Imagine fans equipped with AR glasses that overlay statistics and tactical insights on live play, or even VR simulations that place viewers right on the court, experiencing the sport from the players' perspectives. Such innovations promise to transform viewing experiences, making them more immersive and interactive, potentially creating new tiers of fan engagement that were previously unimaginable.

Moreover, the prospect of intelligent wearables is buzzing within the tennis community. Future wearables could become more sophisticated, offering granular insights into player biometrics beyond what is currently possible. These devices could track stress levels, hydration, and even sleep patterns, providing a holistic view of an athlete's condition. Such advancements could lead to highly personalised training regimens tailored to each player's unique physiology, potentially reducing the risk of injury and extending athletic careers.

The integration of AI with machine learning in predictive analytics promises another ground-breaking shift. Systems could foresee outcomes with unerring accuracy, helping players prepare for matches by potentially knowing the patterns and habits of their opponents better than the opponents know themselves. AI-driven simulations could prepare athletes for the exact scenarios they're likely to face, giving them a strategic advantage before stepping onto the court.

On the administrative side, AI can certainly play a role in spreading tennis to underrepresented communities. By lowering the barriers to entry through innovative solutions such as AI-driven coaching platforms, both seasoned professionals and budding players can access high-quality training regardless of their geographical limitations. AI could also be pivotal in environmental management, optimising energy use in court facilities and contributing to more sustainable tennis ecosystems by predicting peak usage times and automating resource management accordingly.

Imagine AI-driven matchmaking systems that create ideal practice scenarios by analyzing player data to find suitable sparring partners. Such systems could balance competitiveness and learning, ensuring players train under optimal conditions for growth. This kind of matchmaking is not limited to the players on the court but could also extend to pairing practising with specific drills and exercises tailored to target individual weaknesses, thus cultivating a generation of more well-rounded athletes.

In recruitment, AI offers the ability to discover hidden talents at an unprecedented scale. It could sift through countless data points to find the next Roger Federer or Serena Williams, even from remote corners of the globe. By evaluating potential based on extensive performance metrics rather than standard scouting reports, AI can revolutionise how talent is identified and nurtured at every level of the game.

Considering ethical concerns, AI advances must be tempered with mindfulness towards privacy and integrity. The algorithms developed must be transparent, and there must be continuous efforts to ensure the fair and equitable use of AI across all levels of tennis. These innovations, while groundbreaking, must not compromise the core values of sportsmanship and fair play that tennis upholds.

As the innovations continue to unfold, they hold the potential not just to influence but to transform the very fabric of tennis. Each breakthrough offers a glimpse into a future where technology and sport harmoniously coalesce, driving the evolution of tennis into a new era of precision, excitement, and inclusivity. With every court becoming a testing ground for the latest analytics-powered tools, the future of tennis is promising and infested with endless possibilities waiting to be realised.

Chapter 13:
Ethics and AI in Tennis

As artificial intelligence becomes more integrated into the world of tennis, it brings forth a myriad of ethical considerations that must be addressed to maintain the integrity and fairness of the sport. Data privacy looms large, as the vast amounts of personal and performance data collected could pose significant risks if mishandled. There's an ongoing debate about fair play; the introduction of AI into coaching and gameplay strategies could inadvertently create inequality, favouring those with more sophisticated technology access. Mitigating unintended consequences is crucial, as AI's intervention might skew traditional approaches to training and competition. There's a delicate balance to strike—ensuring AI enhances the sport without diminishing the human element that fuels its passion and unpredictability. Navigating these challenges requires a collective effort from governing bodies, tech developers, and the tennis community to establish guidelines that respect both innovation and the game's rich heritage.

Data Privacy Concerns

As artificial intelligence begins to play a more prominent role in tennis, data privacy becomes a critical ethical consideration. In today's game, every stroke, strategy, and even sweat bead can be quantified and analysed through AI tools. Yet, this treasure trove of data, collected from players, coaches, and enthusiasts, poses significant questions about its security and use. How this data is managed not only affects personal privacy but also the integrity of the sport itself.

One of the primary concerns is the sheer volume of information collected by AI-enabled devices. Smart rackets, wearables, and even court sensors gather unprecedented amounts of data, ranging from biometric details like heart rate variability to performance metrics such as swing speed and shot patterns. While these insights can enhance performance and strategy, they also risk being exploited if not properly safeguarded.

Furthermore, there's a need to establish who owns the data generated during a match or training session. Is it the player, the coach, or the organisation that provided the technology? The ownership question is crucial as it determines not only who controls the data but also who may benefit financially from selling it. Players could find themselves unintentionally waiving rights to their own performance data, which could then be sold to third parties without their informed consent.

In addition, the prospect of data breaches looms large over the sport. Data in the wrong hands could lead to competitors gaining an unfair advantage by accessing private profiles, training regimens, and even medical records. The strength and security of data storage solutions become paramount, and strict regulations are necessitated to prevent unauthorised access.

The ethics of data privacy in tennis also intersect with the issue of informed consent. Players, especially juniors and amateurs who might be less acquainted with legal jargon, may unknowingly agree to extensive data collection when they use AI-enhanced equipment. Transparent policies and consent forms should be a standard to ensure that all athletes are aware of what data is being collected and how it might be used.

Beyond player privacy, fans' data is also increasingly collected as AI optimises fan engagement through interactive platforms and personalised content delivery. While this can enhance the spectator experience, it raises the question of how much personal data an organisation can collect and process without crossing ethical lines. Balancing user experience with privacy is critical to maintaining trust.

Current regulations surrounding data privacy in sports often lag behind technological advancements. However, various governing bodies and organisations are beginning to address these concerns. They are implementing policies to ensure that AI is used ethically and that data privacy is preserved. Still, it's an ongoing battle, and there are calls for more robust international standards that can comprehensively govern how tennis addresses these challenges.

Data privacy concerns also extend to scenarios where players might be subjected to unsolicited data-driven evaluations. For instance, an athlete's performance or health could be analysed and critiqued without their permission, thanks to publicly available data or footage. Such evaluations could be exploited for speculative journalism or unwarranted public scrutiny, which could affect a player's mental well-being and public image.

The potential misuse of AI in tennis for surveillance is another ethical issue. Continuous data tracking could inadvertently become a form of monitoring, eroding the players' sense of autonomy and freedom on the court. Such conditions demand a conversation around the ethical limits of data usage to ensure players' dignity and peace of mind are respected.

One innovative approach to tackling these issues could be the implementation of decentralised databases using blockchain technology, which offer greater transparency and control over data ownership. Employing smart contracts could empower players to monetise their data fairly or restrict its use, potentially redefining data privacy norms within the sport.

The rapid evolution of AI necessitates ongoing education and dialogue among players, coaches, and administrators about data rights and privacy. An informed community will be better equipped to navigate the blurring lines between technological innovation and ethical responsibility. Organisations could introduce mandatory workshops to educate stakeholders about data privacy laws and their implications in tennis.

Ultimately, the intersection of AI and data privacy in tennis is a reflection of broader societal challenges as technology continues to advance rapidly. Striking a balance between innovation and privacy will be critical to ensuring the sport not only thrives in a modern context but also remains fair and transparent for generations to come. Implementing robust data privacy standards will uphold the integrity of tennis and protect the rights and freedoms of those engaged with it.

Fair Play and Integrity

As the integration of artificial intelligence into tennis reaches unprecedented levels, questions surrounding fair play and integrity naturally arise. Tennis has always prided itself on the principles of sportsmanship and honour, values echoed in its code and etiquette. But today, as AI systems begin to influence everything from line calls to strategic decisions, it's essential to examine how these technologies align with the ethos of fairness.

Historically, the spirit of fair play in tennis is embedded in both the written rules and the unwritten codes that players and fans have come to cherish. Yet, as technology increasingly mediates every aspect of the game, there's a tangible shift in the landscape. With AI-driven line-calling systems now commonplace, instances of human error that once provided fodder for spirited debate have drastically diminished.

But removing human fallibility does not inherently assure fairness; the algorithms themselves must be free from bias and error, raising a new dimension of ethical scrutiny in technology's deployment.

In this brave new world where AI and sports intersect, integrity checks must evolve. Ensuring that these systems are designed and implemented without prejudice requires transparency and regular auditing. Algorithmic fairness needs to be as much a part of the conversation as rule books and umpire training. There are concerns about implicit biases being embedded within AI, primarily when datasets used for machine learning are not as diverse or representative as they should be. This potential for bias means that continuous oversight and evaluation of AI models are non-negotiable.

While AI technology has transformed line-calling with high precision, even the most sophisticated systems must account for interpretative nuances in complex scenarios. It's crucial that these innovations support rather than supplant human judgement. Each match and moment has unique contexts and subtleties that a purely algorithmic approach might overlook. Thus, the technology must remain a tool to assist decisions, not replace the spirit and human touch that defines tennis.

Integrity isn't solely about accurate line calls; it's about levelling the playing field across all dimensions. AI innovations must be accessible to all levels of competition to prevent an uneven playing field where only top-tier athletes and institutions benefit. Bridging this gap ensures that AI enhances rather than dominates the game. If AI tools are not democratised, they risk exacerbating existing disparities, turning tennis into a game of technological haves and have-nots.

Moreover, the drive for fair play extends to making sure AI does not become a surveillance tool that breaches athletes' privacy. Enhanced performance analytics and biometric monitoring offer unprecedented insights, yet they must be balanced with safeguarding player confidentiality. Clear guidelines and robust data-protection frameworks are needed to maintain trust and uphold the game's integrity.

The ethical use of AI in tennis requires deliberate reflection and action. Technological advancements should be approached with caution, acknowledging their potential for both enhancing and complicating the sport. Advocates for fair play and integrity have the opportunity to work hand in hand with technologists, ensuring that AI in tennis upholds and enriches the noble traditions of the sport.

Part of ensuring fair play involves stakeholder engagement. Players, coaches, technologists, and governing bodies ought to collaborate on creating and maintaining systems that serve the sport's best interests. Establishing ethical guidelines from the ground up, with input from diverse voices, ensures the tennis community remains aligned with the principles of fairness.

The philosophical implications of AI in tennis are as profound as they are practical. By weaving together the ethical threads that underpin fairness, the game can remain true to its roots while embracing the benefits of cutting-edge technology. Forward-thinking governance will be essential—one that navigates between innovation and tradition to safeguard the future integrity of tennis.

In our pursuit of integrating AI into tennis, there's an opportunity to set a global precedent for ethics in sport that transcends tennis itself, possibly influencing other sports' foray into AI. By leading the way with transparency, inclusivity, and fairness, tennis can establish a benchmark that both inspires and guides other sporting communities around the world.

The next phase of tennis, with AI at its helm, hinges on a commitment to these foundational values. The sport is standing at a crossroads where innovation meets integrity; how it proceeds could redefine not only the rules but the spirit of the game itself. Reaffirming a commitment to fair play ensures that AI is not merely a tool for enhancement, but a partner in preserving tennis as a true test of human skill and spirit.

Mitigating Unintended Consequences

As we delve deeper into the fusion of artificial intelligence and tennis, it becomes crucial to address the unintended consequences that may arise. The advent of AI in sport has been transformative, but this transformation comes with its share of challenges. Navigating these complexities demands a comprehensive understanding of the ethical landscape and proactive strategies to counteract potential pitfalls. In this section, we'll explore how to balance innovation with integrity, ensuring AI's role in tennis remains beneficial and fair to all participants.

The rise of AI in tennis presents exciting opportunities, but it can also perpetuate biases. Algorithms trained on biased datasets may unintentionally reinforce existing disparities. For instance, if player performance data predominantly features top-tier athletes, AI systems may overlook emerging talent from less represented backgrounds. This oversight could stifle diversity and reduce the accessibility of opportunities for all players. To mitigate these biases, stakeholders must ensure that training datasets are inclusive and representative of the diverse profiles present in the tennis community.

One of the potential unintended consequences of AI in tennis is the erosion of the human element within the sport. Tennis, like other sports, thrives on human unpredictability, emotion, and spirit. Over-reliance on AI for decisions—be it in strategy or training—may diminish the role of instinct and personal touch that coaches and players bring to the game. To counter this, it is essential to use AI as a supportive tool rather than a replacement. By blending AI insights with human intuition, tennis can preserve its unique character while benefiting from technological advancements.

Privacy concerns are another critical aspect when discussing the intersection of AI and tennis. As wearable technology and data analytics become increasingly integrated into training regimes, the amount of personal data collected grows substantially. Players' performance metrics, health records, and even personal habits may be scrutinised, leading to concerns about data security and privacy. Implementing robust data protection measures and clear data handling policies will be key in safeguarding players' privacy and maintaining trust in AI systems.

The dynamic nature of tennis, with its rapid pace and constant evolution, means that AI systems need continuous updates and monitoring. Outdated algorithms could lead to outdated strategies, potentially misguiding players and coaches. Moreover, technological obsolescence might widen the gap between well-funded teams and those with limited resources. Ensuring equitable access to regular updates and maintenance of AI systems is fundamental to prevent a divide where only certain players can benefit from the latest technology.

Moreover, as AI becomes part and parcel of scouting and recruitment processes, there lies a risk of reducing players to mere data points. While AI can aid in identifying talent by analysing performance metrics, it must not overlook factors like player attitude, potential for growth, and team compatibility—qualities that numbers alone can't capture. A holistic approach combining AI-driven metrics with human judgment could offer a more rounded understanding of player potential, ensuring recruitment processes remain equitable and comprehensive.

Injury prevention and management benefit greatly from AI, yet relying solely on AI-derived insights can pose risks. Predictive models need to be integrated with expert medical opinions to ensure comprehensive player care. An over-dependence on AI can potentially overlook nuanced medical insights that a human expert might discern. A symbiotic relationship between AI tools and human expertise is essential, ensuring a well-rounded approach to injury prevention that considers both data and human insight.

As AI technologies advance, maintaining a level playing field becomes more complex. Automation in line calls, for instance, has improved accuracy, yet perceptions of bias or fault could arise from reliance on machines over human judgment. Transparency in how AI systems operate and decisions they make is paramount to building trust among players, coaches, and fans. Educating all stakeholders on AI's role in tennis could diminish scepticism and facilitate a smooth integration of these technologies into the sport.

Fair play and integrity in tennis can be challenged if advanced AI analytics are restricted to privileged clubs or individuals. To mitigate this, frameworks ensuring equitable distribution of AI technologies must be established. Governing bodies could play a pivotal role in offering grants or subsidies for under-resourced teams, levelling the playing field so that innovations benefit all levels of the sport. This approach not only fosters fair competition but also paves the way for diverse talent to shine irrespective of their financial background.

Ultimately, as tennis continues to evolve and embrace technology, it's imperative that AI's implementation considers the broader social and ethical implications that come with it. By fostering collaboration between technology developers, ethicists, and sports professionals, we can craft AI solutions that elevate the game while respecting its traditions and values. Balancing innovation with responsibility ensures that tennis remains a showcase of not just technological prowess, but sportsmanship, fairness, and human excellence.

As AI becomes further entrenched in the sport, ongoing dialogue will be central to addressing the evolving ethical challenges. This requires a commitment from all stakeholders within the tennis community to continuously review and revise ethical standards as technology progresses. By doing so, they can safeguard the sport from potential pitfalls while capitalizing on the immense benefits that AI offers. A future where technology and tradition harmoniously coexist not only preserves the essence of tennis but also enhances its reach and impact across the globe.

In conclusion, mitigating unintended consequences is an ongoing process that requires vigilance, creativity, and collaboration. The balance between innovation and ethics will ultimately define the future of tennis in the age of artificial intelligence. By taking proactive steps today, we can ensure that AI's influence serves to enrich the sport, maintaining its legacy while paving the way for new generations to experience and enjoy tennis in novel and exciting ways.

Chapter 14:
Cost Considerations and Accessibility

As we delve deeper into how artificial intelligence is revolutionising tennis, it's essential to address the economic barriers that come with these innovations. While AI tools offer unprecedented data-driven insights and performance enhancements, their cost can be prohibitive for many players and clubs. However, solutions aimed at lowering these costs are emerging, driven by advancements in technology and the increasing adoption of AI at all levels of the sport. By embracing scalable AI systems and open-source platforms, we can work towards democratising access, ensuring that players of varying skill levels and economic backgrounds can benefit from these technological breakthroughs. Ultimately, the goal is to create an ecosystem where AI is not just a privilege for the elite but a resource available to enthusiasts and budding athletes, nurturing talent and passion across the globe.

Economic Barriers

In the rapidly evolving landscape of tennis, artificial intelligence (AI) stands as a beacon of innovation, promising to revolutionise every aspect of the sport. Yet, amidst this promise lies a daunting reality—economic barriers that threaten to restrict the transformative potential of AI to a privileged few. The integration of AI into tennis encompasses a plethora of new technologies, from advanced analytical tools to state-of-the-art training devices. These innovations, however, often come with hefty price tags, posing significant challenges for widespread adoption.

AI systems require substantial initial investments in both hardware and software. State-of-the-art sensors, cameras, and computing facilities are not inexpensive, and the costs can escalate rapidly when scaling up from personal use to professional-level applications. For many individuals and small tennis organisations, the financial burden of adopting these technologies can seem insurmountable. This is especially true in regions where tennis is still developing, lacking the commercial infrastructure that supports the sport in wealthier countries.

More than just the upfront costs, the ongoing expenses associated with AI deployment must be considered. These can include software updates, data storage fees, and maintenance charges. As AI technology evolves, continuous investment is necessary to keep systems up-to-date. Moreover, hiring skilled professionals to interpret AI-generated data and integrate it into training or match strategies adds another layer of financial outlay, further exacerbating the economic divide.

The disparity in economic capacity between amateur players, small clubs, and top-tier tennis facilities creates a technology gap that mirrors broader socioeconomic inequalities. While professional players and elite clubs can leverage AI to enhance performance and strategy, those on the lower rungs might struggle to access even the fundamental tools necessary for advancement. This gap raises crucial questions about the democratisation of technology and how the sport can be inclusive while embracing technological change.

It's also imperative to consider the impact of economic barriers on junior and grassroots tennis. For young players in particular, AI could offer unparalleled opportunities for skill development and coaching accessibility. However, the economic constraints faced by many families might prevent them from reaping these benefits. The risk here is not just that potential talent may go unnoticed, but also that the allure of tennis could wane among the youth who see it as a sport for the affluent rather than for all.

In professional tennis, the financial heft of AI-driven tools might be less of a concern given the potential return on investment. Successful players and prestigious tournaments can justify such spending by attracting lucrative sponsorships and increasing fan engagement through technology-rich experiences. However, this economic assurance doesn't extend to smaller tournaments and lower-ranked players who often operate on tighter margins. For them, the challenge is balancing the cost of AI integration with uncertain financial benefits.

The question of economic barriers is not solely about the cost of acquisition but also about the redistribution of revenue within the sport. As AI technologies become intrinsic to the competitive edge in tennis, federations and governing bodies must decide how to balance the scales. Financial incentives, subsidies, or partnerships with technology companies could serve as vehicles for levelling the playing field. In this context, collective action and innovative funding models could pave the way towards broader accessibility.

Besides institutional efforts, individual entrepreneurs and startups are also exploring solutions to democratise AI in tennis. By developing cost-effective models and sharing-based services, these innovators aim to make high-tech tools more accessible. Furthermore, open-source platforms and community-driven projects could reduce entry costs, allowing players and clubs with limited budgets to engage with AI on a level playing field.

Addressing economic barriers also necessitates a cultural shift within the tennis community. Acknowledging that tech advancements should not create exclusivity but instead drive inclusivity is essential. Coaches, trainers, and players must advocate for affordability and accessibility, fostering an ecosystem where growth is not stymied by financial limitations. This means valuing collaboration and shared knowledge over competition and secrecy within the tennis and tech communities.

Moreover, the role of governmental policies cannot be understated in mitigating economic barriers. Subsidised schemes for sports tech innovations or grants for young players could support broader access to AI tools. Governments, understanding the societal benefits of sports participation, may find significant interest in investing in AI's potential to nurture both talent and health in the general population.

Ultimately, addressing economic barriers requires a multifaceted approach. Collaboration between public bodies, private enterprises, and tennis institutions will be crucial in steering the sport towards a future where genuine inclusivity prevails. The potential of AI in transforming tennis and making it more accessible is immense, but realising this potential hinges on overcoming the economic hurdles that currently stand in its way.

As the sport continues to embrace AI, it must not lose sight of its responsibility to all its participants, irrespective of their economic standing. By confronting these barriers head-on, the tennis community can move towards a more equitable future, ensuring that everyone from future champions to recreational enthusiasts can partake in the digital renaissance of this timeless game.

Solutions for Lowering Costs

In the realm of tennis, artificial intelligence (AI) promises to revolutionise how the game is played and experienced. However, these innovations often come with significant costs that could hinder widespread adoption. It's crucial to explore solutions aimed at reducing these expenses, ensuring that both professional and amateur players can benefit from AI technologies without financial strain.

One immediate solution for lowering costs involves economies of scale. As AI technologies become more mainstream across industries, the cost of hardware and software decreases. Tennis can benefit from this trend if organisations approach AI implementation collectively. Shared resources between clubs and associations can drastically lower individual expenditures.

Another approach involves partnerships with technology companies. By collaborating with AI firms, tennis organisations can negotiate better rates for implementation. Tech companies eager to showcase their innovations in sport might offer discounts or sponsorships. These partnerships allow tennis bodies to gain expertise and tools at reduced rates, fostering a symbiotic relationship that benefits all parties.

Additionally, open-source software presents a cost-effective alternative. Utilising publicly available AI tools enables tennis clubs and academies to experiment with advanced analytics and personalised coaching without hefty licensing fees. Open-source platforms also encourage community development, leading to improved tools at no additional cost.

Cloud computing is another solution. Instead of investing in expensive physical servers, tennis organisations can leverage cloud services to host AI applications. This reduces the need for extensive infrastructure, and organisations pay only for the resources they use. Cloud-based solutions also offer scalability, allowing services to grow with user demand without upfront substantial investments.

Training current staff members to utilise AI tools effectively can also be a cost-saving measure. By investing in professional development, organisations can empower existing coaches and analysts to integrate AI insights into their workflows. This reduces the need to hire external experts, who may demand higher fees.

Moreover, the use of AI to optimise operational efficiencies can lead to savings that offset its costs. For instance, AI can automate tasks such as scheduling and court maintenance, allowing clubs to reduce manual labour expenses. These savings can then be redirected towards AI innovation, creating a cycle of efficiency and reinvestment.

Another viable strategy lies in exploring AI solutions tailored for various budget levels. Not all tennis organisations have the same financial capabilities as professional bodies. However, emerging tech companies are developing scalable AI solutions that cater to different economic situations, ensuring accessibility to a broader audience. These tiered solutions maintain essential functionalities while accommodating financial constraints.

Looking at international case studies, we see tennis organisations that have successfully lowered AI costs by engaging in community-driven initiatives. Community-led projects spearheaded by passionate individuals or groups have leveraged local resources and crowdfunding to introduce AI technologies. Clubs around the world have already adopted this model, proving that grassroots efforts can yield high-tech outcomes.

When it comes to funding, government grants and non-profit organisations remain untapped resources. These entities are often willing to invest in sports development and technological advancement, recognising the societal benefits. By applying for funding, organisations can alleviate the financial burden associated with AI integration.

Additionally, customised membership models can distribute costs more equitably among users. Offering tiered memberships with varying levels of AI access allows more participants to experience technology benefits. This approach ensures that even players with limited financial means can enjoy AI-enhanced training and gameplay insights.

Lastly, ongoing research and development in AI technology continue to identify ways to make AI more cost-effective. As algorithms become more efficient and hardware less expensive, the overall investment required diminishes. Staying informed about technological advancements ensures that tennis organisations can rapidly adapt and integrate these improvements as they become available.

By implementing these strategies, tennis organisations can effectively manage costs associated with AI integration. Making AI accessible and affordable will ensure the sport benefits as a whole, enhancing the experience for players, coaches, and fans alike. The future of tennis enriched by AI isn't a distant dream but an attainable reality when approached with innovation, collaboration, and a keen eye for opportunity.

Making AI Accessible to All Levels

Artificial intelligence (AI) stands as a beacon of potential, poised to redefine how tennis is played, coached, and even experienced by fans around the globe. Yet, this transformative power must be harnessed inclusively, ensuring that the advancements in AI don't become privileges for a select few. Making AI accessible to all, from grassroots players to elite professionals, involves understanding and tackling both the economic and educational barriers faced by different stakeholders in the tennis community.

For many, the most significant hurdle in accessing AI technology is the cost. High-end AI systems are often synonymous with expensive hardware, subscription fees, and the need for specialised training. Small clubs and amateur players might find these costs prohibitive, hindering their participation in this evolving tennis landscape. However, progress is being made, as companies begin to adopt tiered pricing models and provide resource-efficient tools that democratise AI technology. AI solutions tailored to varying budgets are crucial in broadening participation and reaping widespread benefits in the sport.

Another challenge in making AI universally accessible is addressing the technological literacy gap. While tech-savvy professionals may embrace AI with open arms, those less familiar with digital tools might find the seas of change tumultuous and challenging to navigate. Educational initiatives aimed at enhancing digital literacy among coaches, players, and administrative staff are paramount. By offering workshops, online courses, and user-friendly AI interfaces, the tennis community can ensure a smoother transition into the AI-era for all its members.

Integration is the key when it comes to making artificial intelligence technology usable and useful for every level. Flexible AI systems that can plug into existing infrastructure without extensive modifications empower smaller entities to embrace technological advancements without overhauling their entire operations. AI-powered video analysis tools, for instance, can be scaled down from professional-grade systems to simple applications accessible from smartphones, allowing players to gain insights from everyday practice sessions at local courts.

Additionally, fostering partnerships between technology developers and tennis organisations can yield innovative solutions tailored to the needs of different users. Collaborative efforts between clubs and tech companies can help customise AI platforms to tackle specific challenges faced in diverse environments, thus making the adoption of AI a more seamless and rewarding process. Through such partnerships, even the most technologically conservative clubs can find themselves effortlessly transitioning into a modern playing field.

In this pursuit of accessibility, creative funding mechanisms and sponsorships could play a pivotal role. Encouraging larger brands to fund AI initiatives at schools or community clubs provides opportunities for underrepresented groups to access premium technology. Moreover, grant schemes aiming at innovation in sport can allocate funds for AI-driven projects that promise to uplift grassroots tennis. Such investments not only enrich the sport but also cultivate the next generation of tennis talent without any socioeconomic exclusion.

It is also imperative to highlight the dual role AI can play: as both a coach and an educator. AI can offer players of all levels insights previously obtainable only through one-to-one coaching. From tracking performance metrics to suggesting fine adjustments in technique, AI systems enhance players' understanding of the game's intricacies and foster an educational pathway that supplements traditional coaching methods. This makes high-level instruction accessible, particularly in regions or communities where expert coaching staff are scarce.

Equally important is the transparent dissemination of information regarding AI's capabilities and limitations. Busting myths and building realistic expectations about AI—such as what it can or cannot do—is essential for nurturing trust and interest in technology adoption across all echelons of the sporting community. Communication strategies should engage not only tech-savvy audiences but also demystify AI for those who may feel apprehensive about its integration.

Finally, a commitment to inclusivity should drive the development of AI systems that respect the diverse needs and aspirations of different tennis players. By embedding values of fairness, transparency, and equity into AI algorithms, technology can become a driving force for social change within tennis. Ethically grounded AI systems should work to eliminate biases and ensure equal treatment, promoting a unified playing environment.

In conclusion, making AI accessible to all levels in tennis is an achievable goal with thoughtful implementation and collective effort.

By addressing economic barriers, enhancing technological literacy, fostering partnerships, creating inclusive funding opportunities, and managing expectations, the potential of AI can be unlocked for everyone. As we continue to advance into the future, these strategies will ensure AI serves as a tool for empowerment, propelling the sport of tennis into a new era of inclusivity and innovation for players, coaches, and enthusiasts around the world.

Chapter 15:
Case Studies in Professional Tennis

In the world of professional tennis, the impact of artificial intelligence has been monumental, serving as both a catalyst for change and a source of valuable insights. From breaking down complex player data into actionable strategies to predicting opponents' moves with mind-boggling accuracy, AI has become an indispensable tool. For instance, the success stories emanating from elite tennis academies showcase how AI-driven training programs have honed the skills of top-ranked players, elevating their game to new heights. Lessons learned from these implementations underline the importance of tailoring AI applications to individual player needs, proving that a one-size-fits-all approach rarely yields optimal results. As we peer into the future, AI offers exciting possibilities from refining real-time tactical decisions to enhancing player health management, indicating that innovation in professional tennis is only just beginning.

Success Stories

Imagine a world where a player's every move on the court is meticulously analysed, not just by coaches but by algorithms that leave no stone unturned. That's the kind of world modern tennis is evolving into, and for many players, this has been a game-changer. AI's integration into tennis isn't just a theoretical exercise—it's translating into real-world victories and substantial improvements in performance, creating success stories that serve as blueprints for the future.

One notable story belongs to a tennis academy that decided to embrace AI-driven training methods in their curriculum. Located in a city teeming with aspiring players, the academy integrated AI video analysis tools, allowing coaches to break down matches frame by frame. Players could adjust their swing or footwork in real-time, thanks to a virtual breakdown that highlighted inefficiencies invisible to the naked eye. After a year of using these techniques, the academy reported a significant increase in their players' match wins. The presence of AI didn't just enhance player performance; it also uplifted the spirits of young athletes facing the challenge of breaking into professional tennis.

At the professional level, players like Serena Williams have expressed how AI-powered wearables are revolutionising their training regimes. Williams, known for her athletic prowess and strategic acumen, used wearables to track biometric data—such as heart rate and recovery times—during workouts and matches. This data enabled her to fine-tune her training schedule, balancing intensity to maximise recovery and minimise injury risks. The result? A season with fewer injuries and more consistent peak-performance moments, illustrating how AI can be both a microscope and a crystal ball in an athlete's toolkit.

Another impressive narrative comes from analysing match strategies using predictive modelling. In a particularly challenging Grand Slam event, a lesser-known player utilised AI-generated strategies to analyse the playing patterns of top-seeded opponents. The AI model provided insights into opponents' weaknesses, suggesting optimal shot selections tailored to exploit them. This player managed to advance further than expected, proving that even when facing unbeatable odds, the intelligent use of technology can level the playing field.

The impact of AI in team environments can't be overstated either. Consider a national tennis team preparing for the Olympics; coaches used AI-driven wearables and real-time analytical tools to complement traditional training. The real-time feedback allowed players to adapt instantly, making tactical decisions on the spot rather than waiting for intermissions or post-match reviews. This approach led the team to a surprise victory, securing medals that initially seemed out of reach.

A success story also lies in the recovery from injuries, where AI has created breakthroughs in rehabilitation processes. A young promising player, once sidelined by a severe ankle injury, followed an AI-based rehabilitation program designed to monitor progress down to the finest detail. This program adapted its recommendations daily, based on monitored healing patterns and the patient's responsiveness, speeding up recovery without risking setbacks. Within months, this player returned to the court, not only healed but with an optimised physical condition that translated into on-court success.

On the scouting and recruitment front, AI's influence has been revolutionary. Take, for instance, a small country with limited resources for scouting athletes. Utilising AI to analyse regional tournaments, scout talent through video analysis, and predict potential based on historic game data has yielded surprising results. Young talent, overlooked in traditional scouting setups, was identified, trained, and ultimately included in national teams. These players became key figures in international contests, illustrating AI's role in uncovering hidden potential.

Moreover, AI has redefined how entire tournaments are approached. For instance, the partnership between a Grand Slam event and a tech company introduced smart courts, where an AI system assisted in match officiating and player scheduling. Real-time data analytics ensured that players' needs were optimally aligned with match logistics, enhancing player performance and event efficiency. This collaboration not only set new standards in tournament management but also resulted in some of the most memorable matches in recent history.

These stories serve as more than anecdotal evidence of AI's capabilities—they're harbingers of what lies ahead. Innovation isn't slowing down. In fact, as technological advancements continue to emerge, these examples will likely become commonplace, setting a new normal that combines human intuition with machine precision. The blend of hard data with human artistry is poised to create a tapestry of success that future generations will aspire to emulate.

As players, coaches, and fans step into this new era, it's vital to recognise the symbiosis AI brings to the traditional elements of tennis. The journey of integrating AI into tennis isn't just about technology—it's about enhancing the spirit of the sport. By learning from these success stories, the community can continue to refine the approach, ensuring that technology serves as an ally rather than a substitute for human ingenuity. We're witnessing the dawn of a paradigm in sport that values data, precision, and innovation, all while honouring the timeless passion for the game.

Lessons Learned

In examining case studies within the realm of professional tennis, several pivotal lessons emerge, shedding light on how artificial intelligence (AI) has significantly transformed the sport. These insights not only showcase the immediate impacts of technology but also offer guidance for future innovations and applications. Intricately woven into the fabric of tennis, AI has redefined player performance metrics and coaching methodologies, while simultaneously revealing unexpected challenges. As we reflect on these developments, it's evident that while AI presents vast opportunities, its integration demands keen strategic implementation.

One of the most crucial lessons learned is the importance of balancing technology with the human element in sport. AI offers unparalleled precision and data analysis, but tennis remains an inherently human game. Players and coaches both thrive on intuition, spontaneity, and emotional resilience—elements that AI can't fully replicate. This understanding emphasises the need for AI tools that complement rather than overshadow human expertise. Integrating AI to empower rather than replace coaches ensures that the sport retains its essence, while still benefitting from technological advancements. This symbiotic relationship between AI and human intuition seems to be the key to optimising training and performance outcomes.

Additionally, AI has revolutionised player performance analysis, enabling coaches to dissect games in ways previously unimaginable. This technological leap has allowed the sport to evolve rapidly, offering detailed insights into player biomechanics, shot precision, and stamina. Yet, the lesson lies in the interpretation of these insights. Successful case studies highlight that the data alone is insufficient; how coaches and players harness this information makes all the difference. The sports professionals who excel are those who can readily adapt analytic insights into practical training adjustments. However, this capability often requires a substantial upskilling to interpret complex data, emphasising the necessity for ongoing education within the tennis community.

From a coaching perspective, AI has enhanced strategic planning by introducing dynamic real-time match strategies. These strategies often surpass any singular coach's ability to anticipate complex variables during a match. However, the effective use of these strategic insights depends on understanding game flow and psychological nuances. Case studies demonstrate that while AI can predict certain outcomes based on past data, the unpredictability of live situations requires human judgement. The ability to meld AI insights with a coach's game-time decisions has proven to be most effective when deploying these advanced strategies.

AI's ability to simulate diverse opponent styles and game conditions also highlights an important lesson concerning player versatility. Preparing players for varied conditions without the need for multiple live matches significantly enhances adaptability. Practicing against AI models of different player styles helps athletes build a robust skill set, preparing them for any opponent. However, there's an underlying humility required—the acknowledgment that AI models are extrapolations, not exact replicas of real-life opponents. This realisation helps maintain an athlete's flexibility and readiness for genuine match play, which often contains an element of surprise and adaptability that AI can't fully encapsulate.

The implementation of AI in injury prevention and recovery presents another insightful learning point. Predictive modelling can foresee potential injuries, allowing for preventive measures and tailored rehabilitation programs. These capabilities not only extend athletes' careers but also enhance their overall well-being. Nonetheless, the effectiveness of these programmes often depends on athletes' engagement and adherence to the suggested routines. Case studies show that the most successful implementations are those where athletes take ownership of their health metrics, proactively engaging with AI-driven recommendations. This collaborative effort between technology and player fosters a culture of health and longevity within the sport.

Beyond individual performance, AI has had a substantial impact on enhancing fan engagement. Personalised content delivery and interactive platforms have transformed the fan experience, making it more engaging and inclusive. Yet, there is a need to ensure that tech-driven experiences do not create a disconnect between fans and the live sport. While virtual reality and interactive elements enrich the viewing experience, maintaining the authenticity and excitement of live tennis remains paramount. The lesson here lies in using AI as a tool to supplement, rather than supplant, the intrinsic thrill of live sports.

Moreover, the lessons gleaned from these case studies also stress the significance of ethical considerations when deploying AI technologies. Ensuring data privacy and maintaining fair play are essential components that need constant vigilance. The credibility and integrity of tennis hinge upon transparent and ethical use of AI. As AI becomes more ingrained in the sport, governing bodies and stakeholders must establish clear guidelines and accountability measures to manage potential ethical pitfalls.

Lastly, cost considerations and accessibility continue to serve as a barrier to AI adoption in tennis. There's an evident need for solutions that democratise access to cutting-edge technologies, ensuring that players and coaches at all levels can benefit from AI. Drawing from successful initiatives, it's clear that partnerships with technology companies can lower economic barriers, making AI tools more accessible. This inclusive approach broadens the talent pool and fosters innovation from grassroots to elite levels, thereby enriching the sport as a whole.

Ultimately, the integration of AI into professional tennis has illuminated a path that balances technology with the indelible human spirit that sports embody. As we consolidate our learnings, future applications will likely revolve around fostering a harmonious co-existence between advanced tech and human skills. This fusion is not just about enhancing game performance; it's about uplifting the overall experience—both on and off the court—for everyone involved.

Future Applications

As we stand at the confluence of AI and tennis, a realm of untapped potential beckons us into the future. The next chapter in professional tennis promises to be transformative, where AI's role is not just a tool but a partner in evolution. This synergy is poised to redefine player engagement, fan experiences, and the strategic fabric of the game itself. In this section, we explore the possibilities that lie ahead, focusing on how evolving technologies could reshape the landscape of professional tennis.

Consider, for instance, AI-powered virtual coaches. Imagine a future where players can access highly advanced virtual trainers that adapt to their unique style and needs in real-time. These virtual coaches could offer immediate feedback during practice, scrutinising parameters like swing speed, foot placement, and even the player's mental focus. This personalised training environment could significantly cut down on learning curves, allowing athletes to reach their peak performances faster. Furthermore, these systems could democratise top-tier coaching, extending elite-level training methodologies beyond geographical and economic barriers.

Looking further, AI's potential in data assimilation and synthesis offers tantalising prospects. Future AI systems might have the ability to absorb vast amounts of data from various sources—match footage, player biometrics, historical performance data—and distill this information into actionable insights with pinpoint precision. This could lead to game strategies that are not merely reactive but predictive, enabling players and coaches to prepare for opponents with unprecedented levels of foresight. Such advancements could radically change the preparation phase of matches, making strategic planning as detailed as the execution itself.

Beyond player applications, AI's future in professional tennis will significantly impact the fan experience. Imagine a stadium experience where AI curates personalised in-stadium activities and real-time match analysis through augmented reality. Fans might use smart devices to access custom stats and information layered onto the live match setting, offering a more engaging and immersive experience. Additionally, AI could revolutionise how matches are broadcasted, offering tailored commentary and highlights according to viewer preferences. The result? A truly engaging fan experience that bridges the gap between the tennis court and the living room.

The application of AI in injury prevention and management is another area ripe with potential. Advancement in predictive analytics could lead to systems that not only warn of impending injuries but also suggest proactive interventions, from altered training regimens to targeted resilience exercises. In the future, AI could integrate seamlessly with wearables to monitor a player's physiological state, offering real-time adjustments to prevent overstrain and facilitate quicker recoveries. This capability to dynamically adapt would not only extend athletes' careers but also ensure they remain at their peak performance levels for longer.

Moreover, officiating in tennis could see further refinement through AI. While automated line-calling systems are already in place, the next step could involve AI-driven adjudication of other in-game elements like foot faults or time violations with extreme accuracy. This would enhance the fairness and integrity of the sport, allowing officials to focus on more subjective aspects of the game that require human judgement.

In terms of infrastructure, the rise of 'smart courts' equipped with IoT and AI capabilities represents a forward-looking vision of tennis facilities. These courts could autonomously manage themselves, from maintenance scheduling to usage tracking, optimising operations and ensuring a top-flight environment for players at all levels. Motion-sensing technologies could also facilitate enhanced security and crowd control, elevating the safety standards for players and spectators alike.

As AI continues to fuse with the sport, collaborative efforts between tech companies and tennis organisations will be crucial. By joining forces, these entities can foster innovative research and drive development initiatives, creating breakthroughs that would have been unattainable in silos. Efforts to promote open data initiatives and grassroots innovations will also be vital, enabling a diverse pool of ideas and strategies to flourish, further enriching the sport.

The next few years could witness a paradigm shift, with AI not just complementing human-led coaching but revolutionising our understanding of how people learn and master complex motor skills. This insight could find applications beyond tennis, influencing how sports are taught globally, with AI-driven modules forming the foundation of training programmes worldwide. As these profound changes take root, the focus will inevitably move towards making these technologies more accessible and affordable across all levels of the sport.

However, the promise of AI in professional tennis will also surface challenges that need prudent consideration. Ensuring ethical standards, maintaining data privacy, and safeguarding the authentic spirit of the game will be critical as we progress deeper into this AI-augmented world. Addressing these concerns through thoughtful regulation and an emphasis on ethical AI use will pave the way for a future where technology enriches, not overshadows, the human element of tennis.

With AI's trajectory in professional tennis mapped promisingly, the future stands to enhance the sport in ways that fuel both competition and admiration. Through diligent integration of AI, the sport could see an era of unprecedented skill, fair play, and widespread participation.

Chapter 16:
AI in Amateur and Junior Tennis

AI's influence is making waves even at the grassroots levels of tennis, providing amateurs and younger players with powerful new tools to elevate their game. Advanced algorithms are now capable of analysing individual playing styles and generating customised insights for beginners, making it easier to grasp the complexities of tennis. Junior development programmes, leveraging AI, are more equipped than ever to tailor training to the unique needs of each player, ensuring that potential is nurtured effectively from a young age. By tracking progress and highlighting areas requiring improvement, these AI-driven tools not only enhance learning but also maintain enthusiasm and engagement. As AI bridges the gap between amateur and professional play, the threshold to elite tennis narrows, creating a new generation of athletes imbued with a heightened understanding of strategy and technique. This democratisation of information and access encourages an inclusive and innovative environment, where talent can flourish regardless of socioeconomic barriers, preparing young players to transition seamlessly into higher levels of competition.

Tools for Beginners

The journey into tennis begins with basic skills and understanding, but even at these early stages, AI is becoming an indispensable companion. Just as seasoned players employ advanced analytics to refine their game, beginners can benefit from AI to lay a strong foundation. The tools designed for this demographic aim to simplify complex concepts, making learning more intuitive and engaging.

One of the most accessible AI tools for beginners is the smart racket. These intelligent devices seamlessly integrate sensors that capture a myriad of data points from each stroke. For a novice player, understanding angles, spin, and racket velocity can be overwhelming. However, smart rackets translate this data into straightforward insights, presenting it in a way that's easy to comprehend. They essentially provide feedback in real time, highlighting areas where changes could enhance performance. Thus, a beginner isn't just left with trial-and-error learning; they have a guide that evolves as they do.

Then there's the role of video analysis—a tool once reserved for the elite is now becoming a common aid for budding players. Beginner-level apps powered by AI offer sophisticated features that can dissect and analyse gameplay frame by frame. These applications use AI algorithms to identify common errors and suggest feasible corrections. The availability of these tools on smartphones and tablets means a player can review their match or practice session almost immediately, empowering them to make tweaks on the fly.

In addition to hardware like rackets and apps, AI-powered coaches are on the rise. These digital assistants can simulate the expertise of a seasoned coach, offering tailored training programs based on the user's input and data collected through practice. By personalising drills and challenges, these AI coaches cater not just to one-size-fits-all routines but adjust to the player's pace and style. This dynamic adaptability is particularly motivating for young enthusiasts who might otherwise feel bogged down by generic training models.

For those just picking up a racket, the concept of biomechanics can seem intimidating. However, wearable technology is bridging this gap with AI-driven biometric sensors. Simple devices like smart wristbands or shoes can monitor biometrics during play. Not only do these tools help track improvement over time, but they also provide evidence-based suggestions to prevent common injuries that novice players might encounter. In doing so, they instil a practice of safety and mindfulness from the outset.

Visualising data is another potent tool that AI offers to beginners. Beyond raw numbers and statistics, AI tools utilise graphs, charts, and animation to convert data into an engaging visual narrative. This is particularly significant for young players who may not yet fully grasp the mathematical side of analytics. By seeing their performance data in colour-rich, animated formats, they can more easily connect actions to outcomes. Visual learning thus becomes a powerful ally, turning abstract figures into tangible results that inspire curiosity and improvement.

Moreover, virtual reality (VR) experiences take the AI offerings for beginners to a whole new level. These platforms allow newcomers to immerse themselves in a virtual court, experiencing scenarios they might not encounter for years in real life. Whether it's practicing serves against a virtual opponent or understanding court positioning, VR tools simulate a variety of match scenarios, helping novices develop spatial awareness and tactical acuity long before stepping into competitive environments. VR is a game-changer, providing a sandbox for experimentation and learning that's free from external pressures.

These AI innovations may initially appear as high-tech luxuries, yet they serve a practical purpose by democratizing access to quality training. Accessibility of AI tools at lower costs encourages broader participation in tennis, diminishing the barriers usually imposed by resource limitations. Scholarships and community programs are increasingly recognising the role of AI, offering access to advanced tools to those who might not otherwise afford them. This shift is nurturing a more inclusive culture, where talent and enthusiasm take precedence over financial constraints.

AI-powered platforms for beginners don't stop at just assisting players; they engage families and communities as well. When tracking progress is so readily visualized and shared, the communal spirit of the sport is amplified. Parents, friends, and local clubs can all become a part of a player's journey, lending support and encouragement as technology bridges geographical and generational divides.

Essentially, the tools that AI offers to beginners are not just about boosting performance—though they effectively do that. They're about cultivating a deeper appreciation and love for tennis, instilling confidence and enabling new players to relish the game at every step. They excite and inspire, turning what can be a daunting mountain of skills to climb into an engaging ascent, complete with thrilling landscapes to explore at every level.

Development Programs

The integration of artificial intelligence in amateur and junior tennis is undeniably transforming the landscape of player development. From the way young players are trained and scouted to how coaches tailor their approaches, AI is playing an essential role. It's not just about elite athletes or top-tier facilities; AI-driven tools are democratizing access to high-quality tennis education, making it feasible for aspiring players at all levels of the game.

Development programs today leverage AI to tailor training regimens suited to individual needs. Traditional methods have occasionally taken a one-size-fits-all approach, tending to overlook the nuanced differences in skill levels, physical capabilities, and learning preferences among young athletes. However, AI offers a robust solution by analysing vast amounts of data, including movement patterns, shot accuracy, and even psychological readiness, to inform bespoke training modules. This personalisation means that each player gets a tailored path to realise their potential, regardless of their starting point.

Furthermore, AI is streamlining the scouting process, which is integral to development programs. Using video analysis and predictive modelling, AI tools are capable of identifying promising talents at the grassroots level with unprecedented accuracy. Scouts no longer rely purely on intuition or subjective assessments; instead, they have access to tangible data that back up their evaluations. This shift ensures that innate talent doesn't go unnoticed and receives the attention it deserves.

In youth development, AI's ability to provide real-time feedback is nothing short of revolutionary. Young athletes often struggle to understand and correct mistakes through verbal feedback alone. AI-powered tools fill this gap by offering visual and interactive feedback mechanisms. For instance, smart rackets equipped with sensors provide instant performance metrics after each stroke, giving players immediate insight into areas for improvement. Combined with digital coaching apps, these tools function as a constant, yet unobtrusive, coach ready to guide the player at any minute.

AI also actively fosters mental well-being in young athletes, an area frequently underestimated in traditional programs. Development initiatives now integrate AI to assess psychological metrics, identifying stressors and areas requiring mental resilience. Unlike previous programs that focused solely on physical efforts, AI-assisted training incorporates mental conditioning, helping juniors build both technical skills and the psychological tenacity required for future challenges.

The affordability and accessibility of such technologies have been a major focus, allowing the benefits of AI to reach a broader audience. Initiating partnerships with local clubs and schools, AI companies aim to implement development programs at reduced costs, providing comprehensive training experiences previously reserved for professional academies. This accessibility paves the way for young talents, regardless of socioeconomic status, to receive advanced training opportunities.

Moreover, the iteration and adaptation facilitated by AI are integral for keeping development programs relevant and effective. As new techniques and insights emerge, AI systems can quickly integrate these into existing training regimens, ensuring that young players are equipped with the latest skills and strategies. Coaches, too, benefit from these updates, as they can adapt their methodologies promptly and confidently, secure in the knowledge that they're providing the best contemporary training solutions.

AI in development programs fosters a community of learning and sharing, where insights are disseminated thanks to cloud-based systems and collaborative platforms. Coaches and trainers from around the world can contribute data and feedback, enriching the AI's database and enhancing its predictive power. This community-driven approach encourages innovation, as practitioners refine and adapt their techniques based on shared experiences and insights.

As AI continues to evolve, its role in tennis development programs will likely expand even further. With the potential of integrating virtual reality and augmented reality into training modules, players might soon experience immersive environments to hone their skills. These advances promise to elevate training to new heights, making learning both engaging and incredibly effective.

The advantages AI brings are numerous, but they must be implemented thoughtfully. Coaches must strike a balance, ensuring technology augment rather than overshadow human elements of coaching. Junior talents, while benefiting from AI, must also develop personal insights and instincts essential for thriving in the dynamic environment of competitive tennis.

Ultimately, the union of AI and development programs is about bridging gaps—whether it's between coach and player, talent and opportunity, or tradition and innovation. As these technologies become an integral part of tennis fabric, they promise not only to redefine how players are developed but also to inspire a new generation of tech-savvy athletes ready to embrace the future of sports.

Bridging the Gap to Professional Levels

In recent years, artificial intelligence has become a game-changer for amateur and junior tennis players aspiring to transition to professional levels. Understanding how to effectively harness the tools and insights offered by AI can play a crucial role in climbing the competitive ladder. It's not just about talent anymore; it's about cultivating a data-driven approach to training that optimises every aspect of a player's development.

AI's capacity to analyse vast amounts of performance data makes it possible to tailor training programmes to individual needs. By leveraging AI-powered technologies, coaches and players can gain insights into key areas such as match play efficiency, swing mechanics, and fitness levels. Such bespoke training regimens allow budding athletes to focus on their weaknesses and fine-tune their strengths, enabling a seamless progression towards professional standards.

The transition from amateur to professional tennis isn't simply a matter of increased skill but involves an intricate understanding of strategy and mental fortitude. Here, AI emerges as an indispensable ally. Advanced algorithms help improve decision-making skills on and off the court, offering strategic insights in real time. Players are better prepared to face highly competitive environments, equipped with tactical foresight that can make all the difference in high-stakes matches.

Another crucial way AI helps bridge this gap is through mental conditioning. AI tools designed to assess psychological metrics allow coaches to understand their students' mental readiness. Stress management apps, powered by artificial intelligence, can aid junior players in maintaining focus and composure under pressure — qualities that are indispensable at the professional level. Imagine a young player stepping onto the court with the calm assurance imparted by AI-guided mental exercises, ready to challenge seasoned professionals.

Additionally, AI-driven scouting reports provide a revolutionary way to identify talent. These reports go beyond mere statistics, providing nuanced evaluations that consider a young player's potential. Coaches can adapt their training plans based on detailed insights that project how an amateur player might fare in different competitive conditions. This allows for a more informed approach to talent development, ensuring that the player's journey is both efficient and effective.

Accessibility to professional resources has historically been a barrier for many players, particularly those from less privileged backgrounds. AI has the potential to democratise access to high-level coaching and analytics. Platforms offering AI-driven training modules are increasingly available, providing experts and young talents with the necessary resources at a fraction of the traditional cost. Devices such as smart rackets and wearable sensors, once exclusive to elite athletes, are now within reach of many aspiring players.

Integrating AI into junior tennis training also facilitates interaction with other technological advancements like IoT-enhanced courts and smart facilities. These intelligent environments serve as incubators for developing talent, simulating professional conditions, and preparing young players for what they will encounter as they advance. The synergy of AI and smart infrastructure creates a dynamic training ground where players can refine their craft with precision and efficiency.

The role of AI in injury prevention has become paramount in ensuring that junior players can engage in sustained training without compromising their physical health. Predictive injury modelling and real-time health monitoring can identify potential red flags before they evolve into serious injuries. These tools offer young athletes the invaluable ability to balance intensity with recovery, thereby extending their career longevity and performance peak.

What's more, AI isn't just changing how players prepare but also how fans engage with these rising stars. As AI-tailored content becomes more prevalent, players achieve personal branding and fan engagement at earlier stages in their careers. Interactive platforms allow fans to follow player progress closely, offering young talents inspiration from the support of a global community. Such interactions can boost the confidence of junior players, motivating them to perform at their best.

In summary, AI in tennis is not merely a trend but a transformative force elevating amateur talents to professional heights. By enhancing every facet of player development—from physical skills to mental resilience—AI ensures a smoother transition through one of the sport's most challenging stages. For the tech-savvy tennis enthusiast, understanding and embracing these advancements is integral to staying ahead in this increasingly competitive field.

Chapter 17: AI's Role in Tennis Commentary and Broadcasting

In a landscape where tennis commentary and broadcasting are continuously evolving, artificial intelligence has emerged as a game-changer, bringing unprecedented depth and dynamism to the viewer's experience. AI enhances live commentary by providing real-time, data-backed insights that commentators can use to deliver more engaging analyses. With AI's capability to automate highlights and generate instant replays, fans are treated to the most thrilling moments without delay. Furthermore, AI enables a personalised viewer experience, allowing fans to receive tailored content that matches their preferences, from specific player statistics to custom highlight reels. This intelligent infusion into broadcasting not only enriches the narrative of each match but also redefines how tennis is consumed, merging technological innovation with the sport's rich tradition. As AI continues to advance, its role in transforming commentary and broadcasting promises an even more immersive and tailored experience for tennis enthusiasts worldwide.

Enhancing Live Commentary

In the fast-paced world of tennis, delivering compelling live commentary is both an art and a science. Traditionally reliant on human intuition and charismatic storytelling, the landscape is rapidly evolving with the integration of AI technologies. Artificial intelligence, with its capacity for real-time data processing and insightful analysis, is enhancing live commentary to new heights. Imagine an experience where insights are not only abundant but also precisely timed and tailored to the viewers' interests.

AI's role in tennis commentating begins with its ability to process vast amounts of data instantly. During a match, multiple variables including player positions, ball speed, and shot types are constantly at play. Historically, commentators relied on their knowledge and instincts to provide expert insights. Now, AI-powered tools augment this expertise, offering data-backed analysis and enriching narratives with statistical depth. This shift provides commentators with a factual backbone, allowing them to paint vivid pictures of the unfolding drama on the court.

One of the most striking changes is the enhancement of statistical commentary. AI can identify patterns and predict potential game scenarios by analysing data from past matches in real-time. For example, when a player has a higher success rate with their first serve in previous matches against a specific opponent, AI can highlight this information, setting the stage for heightened viewer anticipation. Such insights transform the viewing experience, turning it into an engaging blend of drama and analytics.

The integration of AI doesn't stop at numbers and predictions. Natural Language Processing (NLP) algorithms are advancing to the point where AI systems can mimic human speech patterns. This means AI can contribute dynamically to the conversation, providing commentary that aligns with the tone and style of human commentators. It's not just about regurgitating statistics but crafting them into stories that resonate with audiences, enhancing emotional connection to the match.

Consider the utility of AI in handling multilingual commentary. As tennis is a global sport with a diverse audience, linguistic barriers often affect consumption. AI can break down these barriers by offering real-time translations and commentary adaptations in multiple languages. This opens the sport up to broader audiences, increasing the inclusivity of tennis events and ensuring fans worldwide are engaged regardless of linguistic differences.

Furthermore, AI enhances live commentary by tailoring content to the individual preferences of viewers. Using AI-driven personalisation engines, broadcasters can offer customised feeds, focusing on players or statistics that interest particular segments of the audience. For example, a fan fascinated by player movements might receive more detailed commentary on footwork and positioning, while another interested in player strategies could get insights on tactical plays. This personalised experience ensures that each viewer receives a commentary that feels directly relevant to them.

Beyond standardising personal experiences, AI is shaping interactive commentary forums where viewers can query the system about ongoing matches or historical facts in real-time. This transforms spectators from passive viewers into active participants, deepening engagement and fostering a community built on shared enthusiasm and knowledge.

Additionally, AI's potential for enhancing live commentary extends into the realm of augmented reality (AR). Imagine watching a tennis match with AR glasses that display player statistics, ranking changes, and shot trajectories right before your eyes. Such visual augmentation, underpinned by AI, can revolutionise how viewers interact with live sports broadcasts, moving the needle from mere observation to immersive observation.

While many innovations are already in play, the future implications of AI in live commentary remain expansive. As technology evolves, AI systems will likely become even more adept at understanding the intricacies of live sports, perfecting the balance between technical analysis and storytelling. The challenge lies in ensuring that AI remains a seamless tool that enhances human creativity without overshadowing it. As with other innovations, the partnership between AI and human commentators must be harmoniously blended to retain the authenticity and spontaneity that viewers cherish.

In conclusion, AI is not just enhancing live commentary but redefining it. This evolution is not simply a feat of technology but a testament to the endless capacity for innovation within the world of sports broadcasting. The integration of AI transforms a traditional craft into a multi-faceted experience that captivates, informs, and brings fans closer to the action. As AI continues to develop, its role in enhancing tennis commentary is set to become ever more significant, promising an era where every serve, volley, and rally is not just witnessed but truly experienced.

Automating Highlights

In the thrilling world of tennis, where each serve could be a match-defining moment, the ability to capture highlights efficiently is invaluable. Artificial Intelligence has begun to play a pivotal role in revolutionising this aspect of commentary and broadcasting. By automating highlights, AI is not only saving time and resources but is providing viewers with an enhanced experience in ways that were previously unimaginable.

One of the biggest challenges broadcasters face is sifting through hours of footage to pinpoint those golden plays that define matches. Whether it's a stunning rally, an unreturnable serve, or an emotional player reaction, these moments are what keep fans on the edge of their seats. Traditionally, this required a team of editors meticulously reviewing tapes, which was both time-consuming and costly. However, AI-driven systems are now capable of analysing live footage in real-time, identifying and flagging standout moments with incredible accuracy.

AI algorithms can process video data to detect specific cues such as player reactions, crowd noise levels, or even commentators' excited tones, to discern what qualifies as a highlight. This process allows broadcasters to compile highlight reels almost instantaneously. It's not just speed that AI brings into the equation; it's the consistency and objectivity in the selection of highlights that ensures fans get the best content, free from human bias or oversight.

One of the more sophisticated ways AI is automating highlights is through machine learning. By training algorithms on thousands of hours of past matches, these systems learn to understand the nuance of what constitutes an outstanding play. The AI's ability to learn and adapt means it continually improves its accuracy, offering broadcasters a continually refined tool that learns the intricacies of the game over time.

For tech-savvy tennis enthusiasts, the benefits are multifold. Not only does this mean access to perfectly curated highlights, but it also offers interactive opportunities. Imagine a world where viewers can request to see specific plays, player performances, or even create a personalised highlight reel based on certain criteria—such as longest rallies of a tournament or best serves of a particular player. The possibilities are immense, offering a richer, more engaging viewing experience.

AI's automation prowess enhances live commentary too. By compiling real-time statistics and visual data, commentators can be better equipped to provide deep insights into game-changing moments. This elevates traditional commentary beyond the obvious, providing a more enriched narrative that keeps fans informed and engaged. As AI continues to innovate in this domain, commentators might soon lean more heavily on data-driven narratives that enhance storytelling, offering fans a more holistic view of the match.

While there's no denying the transformative impact of AI on broadcasting tennis highlights, there remain challenges and considerations. The implementation of AI solutions requires significant investments in technology and training. There's also the potential risk of over-reliance on technology, which might lead to loss of the human touch, especially the intuitive understanding of context that a seasoned editor can provide. It's a delicate balance between technology and tradition.

Ethical considerations arise as well. Who decides what elements are important enough to make the cut? There is a risk of perpetuating biases that exist in training data, potentially skewing highlight selection to favour certain players or styles of play over others. Ensuring diverse and representative datasets become crucial in tackling these biases.

Despite these challenges, the integration of AI in automating tennis highlights marks an exciting frontier. As technology continues to evolve, the efficiency and capabilities of these systems will only improve, promising unprecedented access to tennis narratives that captivate and enthral. For players, coaches, and fans alike, AI offers a tool that not only captures the essence of the game but also enhances the passion and excitement surrounding those seminal moments that define championships and careers.

In conclusion, automating highlights is just one example of AI's transformative role in tennis commentary and broadcasting. By bridging technology with sports journalism, we are witnessing the evolution of sports consumption into a more interactive and engaging experience, tailor-made for a digital-first audience that craves instant gratification and personalised content. As we continue to explore the vast potential of AI in tennis, one thing is certain: it's a game-changer in every sense of the word.

Personalised Viewer Experience

Artificial Intelligence is revolutionising how tennis fans consume and interact with the sport, creating personalised viewer experiences that were once unimaginable. At the heart of this transformation is the ability to tailor content to individual preferences, making every match feel uniquely engaging and highly personal. The days of generic broadcasting are slowly disappearing, replaced by AI-driven experiences that cater to the intricate desires of each fan. Whether you're a seasoned tennis enthusiast or a casual viewer, the game on your screen can align perfectly with your interests.

Picture this: you tune into a tennis match and immediately the commentary is tailored to your level of understanding and preferred focus, whether it be strategic insights, player backstories, or match statistics. This isn't merely a futuristic dream. AI has the capability to analyse vast amounts of data to offer commentary that not only caters to various interest levels but also dynamically shifts based on the progression of the match. For those hungry for data, real-time statistics and player metrics can be seamlessly integrated into the viewing experience.

One of the key elements driving this change is machine learning algorithms that can profile viewers based on their interactions and preferences. By analysing what types of matches you watch, how often you view certain players, and how you interact with tennis-related content across platforms, AI systems can create a viewing profile that's unique to you. This allows networks and streaming platforms to offer recommendations not just on matches but segments within matches, bringing your favourite players or types of rallies to the forefront.

Moreover, personalised viewer experiences extend beyond what's on the screen. With AI, fans can engage with the sport in an interactive manner. Imagine a feature where you can ask real-time questions about match strategies or player statistics and receive immediate, insightful answers. This interactivity turns passive viewers into active participants, enriching their connection with the sport and providing deeper engagement.

Decisions regarding camera angles are another fascinating area where AI can enhance the viewer experience. Typically, a director decides which camera angles are broadcast during a match. However, an AI system can adapt angles based on a viewer's past preferences. If one prefers close-up player reactions or finds overhead shots more engaging during rallies, the broadcast can adjust accordingly, making the experience feel customised. This technology promises to immerse fans in the match as though they were there in person, and it doesn't just stop at replays; it can happen live.

AI's capability to automate and personalise extends even further with the integration of augmented reality (AR) elements. Viewers can choose to have AR overlays providing statistics such as serve speeds, spin rates, or player trajectory paths. This additional layer of information can be toggled on or off depending on viewer preference, transforming the way we consume live sports and offering levels of insight that were once only available to professional analysts. Imagine watching a match with an instantaneous breakdown of each shot, enhancing your understanding of player strategies.

Another noteworthy development is AI's role in delivering content in different languages and dialects, breaking down geographical barriers and helping to grow tennis's global audience. Automatic translation and localisation of commentary means fans from diverse linguistic backgrounds can enjoy matches with commentary in a language they are comfortable with, further personalising and expanding the appeal of tennis globally.

Social media and community engagement has also been revolutionised. AI technologies can analyse fan sentiment and trends in real time, providing broadcasters with the opportunity to integrate fan opinions and popular topics into the coverage. This becomes a dynamic feedback loop where the preferences and thoughts of the viewer are not only heard but become an integral part of the broadcast. In this way, AI offers a participatory platform where fan voices can influence what aspects of a match are highlighted or discussed.

Despite these advancements, accommodating vast technological sophistication within personalised viewer experiences does not come without its challenges. Ensuring the privacy of data and the ethical use of personal preference information is paramount and requires stringent security measures. As much as AI provides a tailored experience, it must do so while respecting and safeguarding viewer data.

The transformation of personalisation within tennis broadcasting is not just about adding layers of complexity to the viewing experience but also about making it more inclusive and accessible. As AI technology advances, the gap between the insider knowledge of seasoned professionals and casual fans narrows, democratizing how we experience and understand the intricacies of tennis. This evolution holds a promise: to deepen our love for the sport, enrich our engagement, and inspire the next generation of fans by providing them with an experience that speaks directly to their interests.

As we continue to explore these advancements, it's crucial to think of AI not merely as a technological service but as an innovative partner reshaping the landscape of tennis. Personalised viewer experiences set the stage for a new era of sporting entertainment where each match is not just a contest on the court but a unique journey experienced singularly by every fan at home. The possibilities are endless, and the path has just begun. As AI continues to evolve, its role in enhancing the viewer experience promises to push the boundaries of how we watch, understand, and enjoy the sport of tennis.

Chapter 18: Regulatory Framework and AI in Tennis

Navigating the intersection of artificial intelligence and tennis requires a robust regulatory framework to ensure that innovation flourishes without compromising integrity and fairness. Governing bodies must establish clear policies that address the ethical use of AI, focusing on issues ranging from data privacy to the maintenance of competitive balance. There's a pressing need to ensure compliance, not as a stifling constraint but as a supportive structure that protects the interests of players, coaches, and fans alike. As AI continues to transform the sport, future regulations will likely evolve to address new challenges and embrace opportunities, necessitating an ongoing dialogue between technology developers and tennis authorities. Ultimately, the regulatory landscape must foster transparency and trust, enabling AI to be a positive force in the sport while safeguarding its core values.

Governing Bodies and Policies

As artificial intelligence (AI) continues to redefine the landscape of tennis, governing bodies play a crucial role in establishing policies that ensure the fair and ethical use of these innovative technologies. The International Tennis Federation (ITF), the Association of Tennis Professionals (ATP), the Women's Tennis Association (WTA), and various national federations are at the forefront of this regulatory endeavour. These organisations are tasked with the delicate balance of promoting technological innovation while safeguarding the sport's integrity and ensuring a level playing field for all participants.

The implementation of AI within tennis raises several significant questions, particularly concerning data privacy, player rights, and technology's role in decision-making processes. Governing bodies are developing comprehensive policies to address these concerns. These policies not only outline how AI can be utilised but also identify the boundaries within which these systems must operate. The core objective is to prevent any advantage through unjust means and protect player data from misuse. This requires a thorough understanding of both AI capabilities and potential risks, a few governing bodies are still in the process of acquiring.

A significant area of focus is the ethical collection and use of data. Players, coaches, and teams collect an immense amount of information on and off the court. This data is invaluable for enhancing performance and strategizing. However, governing bodies are acutely aware of the risks involved if this data is improperly accessed or utilised. Policies are being formed to enforce data protection standards, ensuring that access to sensitive information is tightly controlled and the rights of players are respected.

Further complicating matters is the international nature of tennis. Since the sport itself doesn't adhere to borders, regulation requires a global perspective. Governing bodies like the ITF are collaborating with regional and national organisations to establish a cohesive regulatory framework. It is crucial for policies to be universally applicable, preventing disparities that could skew competitive fairness. The idea is to create an environment where AI can thrive without overshadowing the sport's human element.

The advent of AI-driven umpiring, through technologies like automated line-calling systems, poses another regulatory challenge.

While these systems significantly reduce human error, they also raise questions about technology's role in officiating. Tennis organisations are tasked with determining the extent to which AI should be involved in match officiation. Policies need to contemplate the impact of AI on the sport's traditional dynamics, ensuring technology is used to enhance decision-making rather than replace the human touch altogether.

AI's integration into coaching and player development is similarly scrutinised. While AI offers immense potential in refining training methodologies and optimising player performance, guidelines are essential to prevent its misuse. Governing bodies endeavour to create policies that facilitate the use of AI tools in coaching while maintaining clear boundaries that preserve fair play. Ensuring that all players have equitable access to these technologies is another area of concern, especially considering the financial disparities between different leagues and players.

Compliance is an ongoing challenge for the enforcement of any policy. Tennis governing bodies are developing compliance mechanisms to monitor and ensure adherence to AI-related regulations. These range from mandatory assessments to regular audits of AI systems used within the sport. Any violation of these regulations could result in penalties or sanctions, underscoring the importance of compliance in maintaining the sport's integrity.

The process of policy-making in this arena is inherently complex, involving continuous dialogue between technologists, sports administrators, and legal experts. This collaboration aims to ensure that policies remain relevant amidst rapidly evolving AI technologies. It's an adaptive approach that is essential for staying ahead of innovations, allowing for swift modifications to regulations as needed. By doing so, the governing bodies aim to future-proof the sport while ensuring that the soul of tennis remains intact.

Looking forward, tennis organisations understand that proactive and anticipatory regulation is imperative. As AI technology continues to evolve and its role in sports becomes more pronounced, policies will need to adapt accordingly. This foresight is vital for preventing potential conflicts and legal challenges that may arise as AI becomes further entrenched in the operational fabric of tennis.

The crafting of AI policies in tennis isn't just about regulation; it's about steering the sport responsibly into an innovative future. It's about protecting the players and the sanctity of the game while welcoming the efficiencies and enhancements that new technologies bring. For tennis to continue thriving in this digital age, it's essential that its governing bodies walk this tightrope with foresight, vigilance, and a deep-seated respect for the game's rich traditions.

In sum, the policies crafted by governing bodies are a testament to their vision for a future where AI complements tennis rather than overshadows it. They serve as the groundwork for a sporting environment that remains true to its roots while transitioning into the next era. The goal isn't just to regulate AI but to make it an ally in the sport's perpetual evolution, ultimately enriching the experiences of players, coaches, and fans alike.

Ensuring Compliance

As artificial intelligence steadily integrates into the realm of tennis, the prospect of ensuring compliance with existing and emerging regulations becomes a critical concern. With AI technologies permeating various facets of the sport, from player development to fan engagement, maintaining alignment with regulatory frameworks ensures not only legal adherence but also preserves the integrity and spirit of the game.

At the core of compliance lies the necessity to balance innovation with traditional values. Tennis, a sport steeped in history, must thoughtfully incorporate advances in AI without overshadowing its core principles. Governing bodies such as the International Tennis Federation (ITF) and ATP have begun setting precedents by establishing policies that both encourage technological innovation and safeguard the sport's integrity. These organisations spearhead efforts to delineate clear guidelines that all stakeholders, from players to clubs, must follow to ensure fair play.

Data privacy remains one of the most significant challenges within the regulatory landscape. AI's reliance on massive datasets, including player statistics and biometric data, raises concerns about how this information is collected, stored, and utilised. Compliance with global standards like the General Data Protection Regulation (GDPR) is non-negotiable, demanding that organisations seeking to implement AI solutions in tennis must institute robust data protection measures.

Despite the inherent challenges, AI offers substantial benefits, demanding a careful approach to compliance that doesn't stifle innovation. To achieve this, there must be ongoing dialogue between tennis authorities, technology developers, and legal experts. These collaborative efforts are instrumental in establishing adaptable frameworks that cater to both the technological landscape and ethical considerations. Such an approach is fundamental to making the sport futuristic yet abiding by age-old ethics.

In addition to data privacy, compliance must address matters related to fair play. Automation and AI-driven systems, such as automated line calling and smart rackets, present potential advantages in terms of accuracy and efficiency. However, they can also introduce disparities if not uniformly regulated. Developing standardized procedures to govern the use of AI across competitions ensures that no player gains an unfair advantage due to technological disparities. Comprehensive certification and auditing of these AI systems by recognised bodies can help in upholding this aspect of compliance.

On the ground, compliance involves rigorous checks and balances that must be maintained. Devices used by players and coaches, such as wearables and smart equipment, should be routinely assessed to ensure they meet established standards. Regular training programs can be instituted to educate players and officials on the ethical use of technology in competitions, reinforcing the values of honesty and fairness.

Another layer of compliance comes from ensuring AI technologies do not detract from the human element of the sport. While AI can assist in strategy formulation and performance analytics, it should not undermine coaches' and players' intuition and decision-making skills. Regulations might stipulate limitations on real-time assists during matches, ensuring that the essence of player skill and strategic acumen remains central to the game.

Moving forward, the adaptability of compliance frameworks will be paramount. With AI being a rapidly evolving field, pre-existing regulations must be amenable to swift amendments. A proactive stance is required, with governing bodies tasked with not only monitoring current interactions between AI and tennis but also predicting future impacts. This foresight allows for preemptive adjustments in policies and avoids knee-jerk reactions to technological advances.

For global consistency, international cooperation amongst tennis governing bodies is beneficial. Harmonising regulations ensures that AI adoption proceeds smoothly and uniformly across different territories, avoiding a fragmented landscape that might hinder international play. Sharing knowledge and experiences between national associations can foster a more unified approach to compliance, leveraging a collective stance against challenges posed by AI.

The role of compliance extends beyond mere adherence to regulations—it's about embodying the spirit of sportsmanship and innovation. By weaving compliance into the very fabric of the sport, AI in tennis can flourish responsibly, delivering on its promise to enhance the game while preserving its lineage. As AI continues to reimagine what's possible in tennis, a solid foundation rooted in robust compliance will ensure that these advances contribute nothing short of positive evolution.

In conclusion, ensuring compliance with regulatory frameworks in tennis when integrating AI technologies is not just a mandate but a commitment to the future integrity and respect of the sport. Guided by both caution and ambition, tennis can harness AI's power while remaining true to its timeless values, crafting a future where machines enhance human triumphs rather than overshadow them.

Future Regulations

As artificial intelligence continues to shape the landscape of tennis, the future regulatory environment will be pivotal in navigating both the potential and challenges posed by this disruptive technology. Foreseeing future regulations is not just about preparing for bureaucratic hurdles but rather sculpting a fair, equitable playing field where the boundaries of human achievement can be justly complemented by machine intelligence. Governing bodies and organisations within the sport of tennis are beginning to lay the groundwork for regulatory frameworks that will define how AI is integrated going forward.

To ensure that AI's intervention in the sport remains ethical and beneficial, future regulations will likely focus on maintaining a balance between human talent and technological enhancement. This balance involves setting limits on how much AI can influence decision-making during matches. As AI systems can analyse player data in real-time and suggest tactical changes, governing bodies might implement rules restricting the extent to which players and coaches can access these insights during live play. Ultimately, these guidelines will preserve the human element that makes tennis so compelling.

Additionally, the aspect of data privacy will play an increasingly crucial role in shaping future regulations. With AI systems collecting vast amounts of performance and biometric data, protecting players' personal information will be vital. Organisations will likely impose stringent regulations to secure sensitive data from misuse or unauthorised access. This could involve defining strict protocols for data storage, sharing, and analysis, ensuring that players' privacy rights are respected without stifling the innovations that AI can offer.

Another potential area of regulation will revolve around the transparency and accountability of AI technologies. As AI systems take on more critical roles—such as officiating line calls and monitoring player health—clarity on how these systems reach decisions becomes paramount. Future regulations might require AI developers to provide detailed explanations of their algorithms and processes, enabling those affected by AI decisions to understand and, if necessary, challenge the outcomes. Transparency will not only build trust among players and fans but also ensure that AI technologies enhance the integrity of the sport, rather than diminish it.

Regulations concerning the inclusivity and accessibility of AI advancements will also need consideration. Tennis, while global, remains a sport with disparities in access to resources. As AI technologies become integral parts of training and performance, ensuring equitable access to these tools should be a top priority. Future regulations might mandate certain AI tools to be made available at subsidised rates for grassroot initiatives or in regions where resources are limited. The goal would be to democratise the benefits of AI, allowing all players, regardless of their socio-economic background, the opportunity to enhance their game.

International collaboration will be critical in shaping these regulations. Tennis, as a global sport, operates under numerous organisations and cultures, each with unique perspectives on technology's role in sports. Developing global standards for AI in tennis will require dialogue and cooperation between different governing bodies, ensuring that established regulations are comprehensive and unified across the board. These collaborations might foster exchange programs, where technological and regulatory insights are shared globally, ensuring that the sport progresses uniformly.

Ethics will remain at the heart of future regulatory frameworks. The use of AI in sports prompts crucial questions about the essence of competition and meritocracy. As AI tools become more advanced, the line between enhancement and unfair advantage could blur. Governing bodies will need to continuously revisit and revise regulations that maintain the spirit of fair competition, ensuring that AI acts as a tool to unlock human potential rather than overshadow it.

Looking into interactions with technology companies, future regulations might stipulate how tennis organisations can collaborate with AI developers. As these partnerships become more frequent, regulations could define terms and agreements to prevent conflicts of interest. Organisations might be required to remain impartial when implementing AI systems, avoiding sponsorships or partnerships that could favour particular technologies over others. These rules would serve to maintain the sport's integrity, emphasising equal opportunity for technology providers through transparent procurement processes.

Moreover, the regulatory framework will have to be dynamic, adapting continuously as AI technology evolves. AI's rapid advancements mean that regulations could quickly become outdated if not regularly reviewed and adapted. Continual learning and agile regulatory practices will be crucial in ensuring that policies reflect current technologies and anticipate future developments. This might involve setting up dedicated AI oversight bodies within tennis organisations, tasked with monitoring technological trends and suggesting regulatory adjustments as needed.

The future regulatory landscape for AI in tennis presents both a challenge and an opportunity to redefine the rules of engagement within the sport. Relying solely on traditional regulatory approaches would not suffice; instead, a proactive, transparent, and collaborative approach is needed. While the journey to establish these frameworks may be complex, the immense potential rewards—in terms of fairer, more captivating competitions and broader access to cutting-edge technologies—make it an endeavour worth pursuing.

Chapter 19:
Collaborations and Innovations

In the realm of tennis, where tradition meets technology, the symbiosis of innovation and collaboration is reshaping the landscape. The journey begins with partnerships between tech giants and tennis organisations, aiming to push the boundaries of what's possible on the court. These alliances have birthed groundbreaking tech, like AI-driven analytics enhancing player performance and fan engagement, emblematic of the sport's transformative future. Beyond high-profile partnerships, grassroots initiatives are nurturing creativity at all levels, fostering an innovative spirit among upcoming talents and local clubs. Collaborative research projects, too, are forging new paths, combining academic rigour with practical application to tackle challenges unique to tennis. Such endeavours not only invigorate the sport with cutting-edge advancements but also ensure sustainability by inspiring a new generation of tech-savvy enthusiasts. Together, these collaborations underscore a shared vision of elevating tennis into the future while honouring its storied past. With each innovation, the boundaries of the game are pushed further, creating a dynamic interface where legacy and modernity coexist and flourish.

Partnerships between Tech Companies and Tennis Organisations

In the ever-evolving domain of sports, tennis stands as a beacon of tradition seamlessly intertwined with modern innovation. As technology continually reshapes the landscape, partnerships between tech companies and tennis organisations have burgeoned, heralding a new era for the sport. These collaborations leverage artificial intelligence to enhance gameplay, refine strategies, and elevate the spectator experience. By pooling resources, expertise, and creativity, these partnerships are creating a synergy that is transforming tennis from courtside to the boardroom.

Tech firms are not strangers to the world of innovation. Their quest for developing cutting-edge solutions perfectly aligns with the needs of tennis organisations searching for novel ways to optimise player performance and fan engagement. When companies like IBM, Google, and SAP join forces with the likes of the ATP, WTA, and various Grand Slam tournaments, the focus is not just on solving immediate challenges but also on envisaging the future of the sport.

At the forefront of these partnerships is the use of AI in performance analytics. In collaboration with tech companies, tennis organisations have employed AI to parse through vast datasets, offering insights previously unattainable through human analysis alone. By analysing player movement, shot selection, and match conditions in real-time, AI systems provide a wealth of data that coaches, players, and analysts can use to their advantage. These collaborations have led to the creation of platforms that integrate data streams, turning raw information into strategic goldmines.

Moreover, the influence of these partnerships extends beyond the professional circuit to the grassroots level. Many tech companies are involved in initiatives that provide AI tools to academies and local clubs, democratising access to high-level tennis analytics. This is especially transformative for players in remote or underserved regions, giving them tools that can bridge the gap to professional standards. By lowering entry barriers, these collaborations strive to nurture talent and foster growth in the sport at every level.

Another crucial area where tech companies and tennis organisations are collaborating is in fan engagement. The modern tennis spectator craves an interactive experience, and AI-driven platforms are stepping up to the challenge. From personalised content delivered through apps to augmented reality features during live matches, these innovations keep fans connected with the sport in unprecedented ways. Interactive systems powered by AI can predict match outcomes, offer statistics, and even allow fans to engage with each other over shared real-time data. Companies like IBM have partnered with Grand Slam tournaments to introduce AI commentators, analysing every stroke and strategy with precision and providing insights during live broadcasts.

The partnerships also bring tangible improvements to the operational side of tennis events. For instance, automated systems for line calling and player tracking are now staples in many tournaments, thanks to collaborations with tech companies specialising in IoT and AI solutions. These systems enhance the accuracy of officiating, reducing controversies and ensuring fair play. Such innovations also accelerate game processes, benefitting players and audiences alike.

Yet, with all these advances, the human element remains paramount. Tech companies and tennis organisations are keenly aware that AI serves best as a complement rather than a replacement. Insights gleaned from AI are tools for coaches and players but don't substitute the intuition and creativity inherent in human decision-making. The aim is to empower individuals to make informed decisions, not to undermine their role in the sport.

The financial implications of these partnerships cannot be understated. By investing in AI development and integration, tech companies gain valuable exposure and credibility within the sports industry, while tennis organisations benefit from technological enhancements that attract new sponsorships and revenue streams. This symbiotic relationship ensures that both entities can push the boundaries of what is possible in sports technology.

However, challenges persist. Aligning the objectives and expectations of different entities requires careful negotiation and strategic alignment. Concerns about data privacy and ethical considerations also surface when dealing with AI technologies, necessitating stringent regulatory frameworks. Both parties must work collaboratively to address these issues, ensuring that the sport's integrity is upheld while innovation flourishes.

Through these partnerships, tennis is witnessing a renaissance of sorts—an infusion of technology that respects its rich heritage while ushering in innovative practices that promise to future-proof the sport. As tech companies and tennis organisations continue to collaborate, one can only anticipate the new horizons they will explore together in this journey.

In conclusion, the partnerships between tech companies and tennis organisations are pivotal in pushing the boundaries of the sport. By embracing AI and other technologies, they are not only enhancing the current state of tennis but are also paving the way for future innovations. It's an exciting time for tennis, with the promise of a game that's smarter, more engaging, and accessible to all.

Collaborative Research Projects

At the heart of tennis innovation lies a dynamic nexus where technology and tradition converge: collaborative research projects. These initiatives often serve as the crucible for groundbreaking advancements, melding the expertise of tech giants with the specialist insights of tennis professionals. Through these collaborative ventures, we witness the transformation of hypothetical scenarios into palpable realities that shape the court and enhance the overall experience of the sport.

Collaborative research projects play a pivotal role in exploring the myriad potentials of artificial intelligence in tennis. By merging academia with industry expertise, these projects harness the collective intellectual power and technical skills to push boundaries. Take, for instance, projects focusing on predictive analytics. By uniting data scientists with seasoned coaches, teams can develop sophisticated algorithms that anticipate player fatigue, enhancing training regimens and potentially averting injuries before they occur.

This symbiosis between tech companies and tennis organisations is further exemplified in projects centred around real-time match analysis. Advanced tracking technologies, built in collaboration with AI specialists, have unleashed a new era of statistical insight. By analysing player movements, shot patterns, and even weather conditions, these initiatives allow coaches to tailor strategies that are responsive to minute-by-minute changes during matches. The impact is tangible, offering a level of strategic depth previously inaccessible.

In seeking to revolutionise player training, several collaborative efforts have focused on smart equipment and wearables. Projects like these have democratised training data, offering insights traditionally reserved for elite players to amateurs and juniors. This encompasses smart rackets that report on swing speed and angle, and wearable devices that monitor biometrics. When leveraged effectively, these tools can highlight performance inefficiencies and inform personalised training programmes.

The success of these ventures often relies on an unwavering commitment to ongoing innovation and adaptability. Initiatives such as the development of automated line-calling systems illustrate the potential for significant advancements. By working alongside regulatory bodies, collaborative projects ensure that technology validates rather than disrupts the spirit of fair play. Such projects not only refine the accuracy of line calls, but also alleviate disputes, thereby preserving the integrity of the sport.

Beyond the clay courts and grassy fields, these collaborative research projects extend to fan engagement. By tapping into interactive platforms and AI-driven content personalisation, they enable a tailored viewing experience. Tech companies and media outlets collaborate to create virtual reality environments that bring fans closer to the action, offering a unique blend of immersion and interaction. Consequently, these ventures fortify the connection between the sport and its enthusiasts, creating vibrant, engaged communities.

Arguably, the most profound collaborations are those that address tennis's intrinsic challenges, such as injury prevention. Projects geared towards predictive injury modelling utilise AI to flag potential risks based on a player's performance data. This proactive approach doesn't solely benefit professional athletes. Widespread implementation can trickle down to grassroots levels, fostering a culture of awareness and injury prevention. When tech experts join forces with medical professionals and athletic trainers, the resulting synergies contribute to a healthier, more resilient player base.

Collaboration isn't without its challenges. Harmonising the distinct cultures of tech and sports often requires methodical negotiation and sustained dialogue. The end goal must always remain in sight: to leverage technology as a tool that complements, rather than replaces, the human aspects of tennis. Projects must keep the sport's traditions and values intact while embracing transformative possibilities.

Looking forward, the promise of collaborative research projects in tennis is both exciting and expansive. Continued partnerships could see AI refining mental conditioning techniques, offering players tailored psychological insights and stress management tools. Furthermore, partnerships might explore the ethical dimensions of embracing AI, ensuring data privacy and maintaining transparency. By addressing such concerns proactively, these projects support an ethical deployment of AI technologies within the sport.

In essence, the forward journey of tennis lies in the seamless fusion of human ingenuity and technological prowess. As collaborative research projects continue to evolve, they stand as testaments to the incredible feats that can be achieved through partnership. They manifest a shared vision of progress that transcends individual limitations, fostering an environment where innovation flourishes alongside tradition. The possibilities are as vast as the imagination— and it is this spirit of collaboration that will certainly propel the future of tennis into uncharted territories, enriching the game for players, coaches, and fans alike.

Grassroots Innovation Initiatives

Grassroots innovation initiatives in tennis are paving the way for a transformative shift in how the sport is accessed, played, and appreciated at community levels. With the integration of artificial intelligence, these efforts are no longer confined to major tournaments or elite training facilities; rather, they permeate community courts and local clubs, making cutting-edge technology reachable to all. The domino effect of this inclusivity is a democratisation of tennis where talent can be unearthed and nurtured, regardless of geography or socio-economic status.

AI-driven grassroots initiatives exemplify how advanced technology can invigorate traditional sports structures. At local clubs and community centres, AI has found practical applications that offer new modes of engagement. With affordable smart devices and apps, even amateur players and budding enthusiasts can gain unprecedented insights into their games. Tools that were once accessible only to top-tier athletes are now available on a modest budget, encouraging broader participation and engagement.

The landscape is changing, particularly in the way young players are introduced to the sport. AI-powered training apps now provide personalised training exercises, catering to individual strengths and weaknesses. These tools can analyse a player's swing, footwork, and agility, providing instant feedback and development plans. The power of AI doesn't just lie in data; it's in turning that data into actionable insights that are easy to follow, encouraging continuous learning and improvement.

Grassroots initiatives are no longer just about getting rackets into hands; they have evolved into cultivating environments where young players feel inspired and enabled. Enhanced by AI, interactive learning modules promote competitive spirit without overwhelming young athletes. For instance, virtual reality platforms allow a kid to feel like they're playing in Wimbledon, fuelling dreams and ambitions, while motion-sensing technology challenges them to improve their tactical game.

An example of this thriving innovation is in community tournaments where AI integration is starting to take hold. Smart scoring systems and automated video analysis allow organisers to run events efficiently while providing participants with detailed performance reports. This level of engagement at grassroots tournaments can dramatically improve players' understanding of their own game, making these events not just competitions but educational experiences.

Furthermore, collaborative projects between technology companies and local tennis organisations are fostering talent discovery. AI-driven scouting tools aim to unearth potential in players who might otherwise have remained unnoticed. By analysing thousands of matches and practices, AI can identify key performance indicators that distinguish a promising talent. This approach allows coaches and clubs to focus resource-intensive scouting on the most promising players, ultimately broadened by AI insights.

Coaching systems are also experiencing a paradigm shift. Where traditional coaching might have relied heavily on subjective assessment, AI provides an empirical foundation where decisions and feedback are data-supported. Smart courts and AI-based systems allow community coaches to plan sessions based on more than instinct, equipping them to focus on correction and encouragement precisely where it will be most effective.

The feedback loops created through AI are not just one way. As more data is collected from local play, AI systems grow more accurate, feeding that data into larger pools that influence higher-order innovations at the elite levels. This synergy ensures that the entire ecosystem of tennis evolves cohesively, with grassroots feeding the professional sphere, and vice versa, for continuous advancement.

Socio-economically challenged areas, often overlooked in the context of technology-infused sport, witness AI breaking down traditional barriers. Community clubs in various countries are using AI to keep kids engaged in sports, offering them a path away from potential negative influences. The increased accessibility to this technology enables clubs to run with minimal resources, reaching hundreds of children without extending financial burdens.

Grassroots efforts also highlight how AI may facilitate social inclusion. Programs focused on involving underrepresented groups in tennis are utilising AI to track and assess organisational impact. Through detailed statistical analysis, organisations can modify and improve their reach, ensuring that inclusivity is not just an aspiration but a growing reality.

The integration of AI in grassroots initiatives embodies the transformational capacity of technology in levelling the playing field, literally and metaphorically. It's a celebration of how AI can bridge divides, offering everyone—regardless of background—an opportunity to pursue their passion for tennis. A new chapter is being written in grassroots sports where opportunity and technology harmonise, crafting tales of growth, achievement, and community spirit.

Chapter 20: Myths and Realities

As artificial intelligence gains prominence in the world of tennis, it's crucial to separate fact from fiction and understand what AI can genuinely offer. One common misconception is that AI will completely replace human coaches and strategists, reducing the sport to cold calculations. In reality, AI serves as a powerful tool that complements human expertise, providing data-driven insights that enhance intuition and experience rather than overshadowing them. The notion that AI solutions are overly complex and inaccessible is another myth; in contrast, many AI-driven tools are designed with user-friendliness in mind, tailored for everyone from professional coaches to amateur players. Crucially, AI doesn't eliminate the unpredictable essence of tennis; rather, it provides a lens through which to examine the game in unprecedented detail. By debunking these myths and setting realistic expectations, we can appreciate AI's true potential: enriching the sport we love by pushing the boundaries of player performance and transforming training methodologies for future generations.

Common Misconceptions about AI

Artificial Intelligence (AI) in tennis is often shrouded in myths, some of which could cloud its transformative potential. One common misconception is that AI seeks to replace human intuition and creativity in the sport. Critics argue that relying on data-driven insights compromises the instinctual and emotional elements that are integral to a tennis match. However, AI is more of a tool than a replacement. It's here to assist players and coaches in making better decisions, not to dictate every move. Think of AI as a complement to human expertise and intuition, an enhancement rather than a substitute.

Another misunderstanding arises around the topic of AI 'magic', where its capabilities are exaggerated. Some advocates portray AI as a flawless oracle, predicting match outcomes and player performances with unerring precision. In reality, while AI offers significant advantages in analysing patterns and trends, it usually operates on probabilities rather than certainties. The dynamic nature of live sport means that the unexpected will always play a part, and AI systems can't account for every variable. Weather, player mindset, or even the pressure of a championship point—these influential factors defy strict data analysis and must be considered alongside AI's guidance.

There's also a prevalent belief that AI accessibility and benefits are confined to professional settings, leaving amateur and grassroots players in the lurch. In truth, AI tools are increasingly being democratized, accessible through smartphones or affordable wearables. Even budget-friendly programs are emerging, aimed at improving the game for players at all levels. The trajectory is clear—technology is gradually permeating all tiers of tennis, blurring the lines between elite and everyday players. Democratization of AI is a reality, opening doors to innovation on local courts far removed from centre-court spotlight.

Privacy concerns sometimes overshadow discussions about AI in tennis. Critics fear the intrusive nature of constant monitoring and data collection, raising alarms about potential misuse. While these concerns are valid and deserve attention, it's important to highlight the rigorous data protection policies being developed and implemented. Regulations and guidelines are continually evolving to ensure that technology is employed ethically, respecting the privacy of all involved.

Game, Set, AI

In many cases, the benefits of AI in improving player safety, injury prevention, and performance enhancement underscore a balanced approach to the privacy debate.

The notion that AI might alienate traditional players from the game has gained traction. Purists worry that reliance on algorithms and machine learning might disconnect players from the elemental joys of tennis. However, most cutting-edge AI implementations are designed to fade into the background, enhancing training and performance imperceptibly. AI's objective is to enrich the sporting experience, allowing players to focus more on the game itself. By managing nuances such as real-time feedback and optimizing training regimens, AI affirms its role as a valued ally rather than an intrusive overseer.

Shifting the lens slightly, some believe AI in tennis exacerbates economic imbalances, making high-tech training accessible only to wealthier players or clubs. Yet this view overlooks initiatives aimed at inclusivity, where federations and organizations are actively engaging in collaborative projects to lower costs. Charitable partnerships, government support, and innovation in low-cost technology are steadily bridging these divides. While it's true that some disparities remain, there's undeniable progress towards making AI a level playing field advantage.

Furthermore, there's a misconception that AI solutions provide immediate, off-the-shelf fixes for complex tennis issues. While AI speeds up processes and improves precision, it requires significant customisation and calibration specific to each player's style and needs. Integrating AI effectively demands commitment from coaches and players in understanding and interpreting results. It's not merely a plug-and-play solution but a component of a multi-faceted strategy to elevate performance.

Then, there's the myth of AI-induced rigidity. Some fear that overemphasis on AI analytics might stifle creativity and player individuality. However, AI's predictive capabilities are about offering alternatives rather than dictating absolutes. By understanding patterns and tendencies, players gain the freedom to explore innovative approaches they might not have considered otherwise. It becomes a catalyst for creativity rather than a constraint.

Lastly, let's address the fear of an AI-controlled future where humans are sidelined. In the context of tennis, AI's role is firmly collaborative. Coaches, analysts, and players are essential in interpreting data and making informed decisions. The human element remains irreplaceable. AI assists by reducing guesswork, but it's the human ability to draw on experience, emotion, and instinct that ultimately defines success.

In summary, it's important to approach AI with a balanced perspective, recognising both its potential and its limits. Dispelling these common misconceptions allows a clearer, more realistic understanding of AI's position within tennis. By doing so, the sport can harness AI's benefits to foster growth, innovation, and fairness, while maintaining the essence of what makes tennis a beautiful, multifaceted game. Such clarity ensures AI serves the great game of tennis, empowering those who wield it to achieve new heights.

Debunking Myths

The intersection of tennis and artificial intelligence (AI) has been a topic filled with both excitement and scepticism. While it's undeniable that AI is a powerful tool, myths have cropped up around its abilities and effects on the game. The need to separate fact from fiction is essential not only for clear understanding but also for fostering innovation without misconceptions holding us back.

One of the common myths is that AI will replace human coaches. While AI indeed provides insights through data-driven analytics, it is only a complement to human expertise rather than a substitute.

Tennis, like any sport, thrives on human elements such as intuition, emotional intelligence, and nuanced understanding—qualities that algorithms simply can't replicate. AI enhances decision-making by offering objective data, but the final call still rests with the coach who can interpret those insights in the context of a player's unique circumstances.

An equally prevalent myth is that AI can predict match outcomes with absolute certainty. While predictive modelling has come a long way, tennis matches are not predictable algorithms. Variables like player form, psychological state, and external conditions contribute to an unpredictable and dynamic sporting landscape. AI predictions are probabilistic, not deterministic, offering insights into potential scenarios rather than certainties.

Some purists argue that AI destroys the essence of the game, turning it into a science rather than an art. The fear is that with data and analytics driving strategies, creativity and flair might take a backseat. On the contrary, AI encourages creativity by freeing players from routine decision-making and allowing them to focus on developing new techniques. AI tools can help identify new shot patterns or strategies that were previously unnoticed, pushing players to test new limits and evolve their gameplay.

The misconception that AI-based tools are only accessible to elite athletes is another barrier that needs dispelling. While it's true that high-level systems can be complex and costly, technology providers are steadily working towards making these tools more affordable and accessible. This democratization of AI technology is instrumental in advancing grassroots tennis, offering benefits to amateur players and local clubs as well.

Another point of contention is the assumption that AI invades privacy, raising ethical concerns around data interpretation and usage without consent. The reality is that AI implementation in tennis is bound by stringent regulations, focusing on ethical standards and data confidentiality. Transparency in data collection and usage is paramount, and most AI systems in sports operate with the athletes' consent, focusing on improving performance rather than exploiting private information.

The belief that AI can completely eradicate human error from match officiating often stems from a lack of understanding about AI's capabilities. Automated systems like Hawk-Eye have indeed improved accuracy in line calling, but they aren't infallible. Technological glitches and limitations still exist, requiring human oversight to ensure fairness and accuracy. The human element in sports officiating remains vital for those moments where interpretation and understanding of context are key.

There's also a myth that implementing AI in training implies a steep learning curve. While initial integration may present challenges, many AI tools are designed to be user-friendly, prioritising intuitive interfaces that even tech novices can navigate. Comprehensive support and training programs are often available to aid coaches and players in making the most of these advanced systems, facilitating a smoother transition.

The assumption that AI-induced improvements translate to instant success is yet another misconception. AI offers tools for enhancement, but dedication, practice, and resilience remain essential components of any player's journey to success. The journey to mastery involves a nuanced blend of AI insights, consistent effort, and the drive to keep pushing boundaries.

Another myth pertains to the idea that the AI-driven focus on metrics and analytics could overshadow the emotional and psychological aspects of tennis. The truth is, AI can be instrumental in mental conditioning by tracking psychological metrics that were once elusive. It enables a holistic approach where both the physical and mental states of players are addressed, harmonising technical proficiency with mental resilience.

Some envisage an AI-dominated future where traditional roles within tennis ecosystems become obsolete, envisioning a world where robots coach, play, and analyze the sport in entirety. However, AI's current trajectory is one of augmentation rather than elimination, supporting each role with unprecedented insights and efficiencies while celebrating the human touch at the core of tennis.

Finally, a word on innovation: The myth that AI stifles creative expression is often unfounded. Instead, AI serves as a catalyst for new creative potentials. The insights garnered from AI analysis can lead to novel strategies and styles that were previously undiscovered. The dance between human creativity and artificial intelligence is one that promises not homogeneity, but a richer tapestry of styles and skills on the court.

Ultimately, the myths surrounding AI in tennis, while understandable, unjustly overshadow the tangible benefits these technological advancements unfold. By dispelling these myths, we can focus on harnessing AI's full potential, ensuring that it empowers players and coaches alike to explore new realms of excellence, all while preserving the integrity and joy of the sport we cherish.

Clarifying Realistic Expectations

As artificial intelligence makes deeper inroads into the game of tennis, it's easy to get swept up in the techno-optimism that often accompanies new innovations. But for all its transformative promise, it's crucial to establish clear and realistic expectations about what AI can, and cannot, achieve in the realm of tennis. Setting pragmatic goals begins with dissecting AI's capabilities while acknowledging its limitations. This allows players, coaches, and fans to embrace these technologies judiciously, without forsaking the human elements that make the sport so captivating.

One of the common misconceptions is that AI will almost instantly produce better athletes or revolutionise playing strategies overnight. The reality is that AI serves as a tool—a powerful one but not a substitute for human effort and intuition. Algorithms can sift through hours of match video and extract valuable insights, but these need to be interpreted and applied by coaches and players. While AI provides data-driven insights, the expertise of seasoned professionals remains indispensable for tactical decisions and player development.

Moreover, AI's power is contingent on the quality of the data it's fed. Biometric devices and court sensors can generate an extraordinary amount of data, but not all of it is useful off the bat. Cleaning, structuring, and interpreting this data demand expertise often glossed over in discussions about AI's magic touch in tennis. It's also important to consider that data collection, especially at an amateur level, might not have the scope or accuracy required for high-level AI applications. This gap can lead to expectations not aligning with on-court realities.

AI won't eliminate the unpredictability of tennis, a sport that thrives on moments of spontaneous brilliance and on-the-fly adjustments. Take, for example, a player known for their flamboyant but inconsistent shot choices. AI might suggest less risky plays based on statistical probabilities, but such suggestions could stifle individual creativity and flair. Coaches and players need to strike a balance, using AI as a support system rather than a directive.

For fans, AI enriches the viewing experience with real-time statistics and personalised content. It offers insights into matches that can deepen understanding and appreciation of the game. However, the risk lies in an over-reliance on these metrics. Stats can tell how many backhands were hit cross-court, but they might not capture the emotional weight of a crucial game point saved through sheer will and determination. Emotional narratives must continue to complement data to maintain the sport's allure.

Then there are practical considerations like cost and accessibility. Cutting-edge AI technologies and devices tend to be expensive, putting them out of reach for many outside the realms of professional tennis. While AI has the potential to democratize tennis by making high-level analysis available to wider audiences, especially through mobile apps and affordable wearables, economic barriers still persist. Bridging these divides is essential to allow players at all levels to benefit from AI's advancements.

Ensuring realistic expectations also involves addressing ethical concerns. Data privacy, for instance, remains a pressing issue as AI systems collect vast amounts of personal data. Players must be aware of how their data is used and who has access to it. Furthermore, maintaining fair play and integrity is critical as AI's role in decision-making grows. Striking a balance between technological advancement and traditional values protects the spirit of competition that defines tennis.

Looking ahead, it's clear that AI will continue to evolve, presenting both opportunities and challenges. Staying informed and adaptable is key to benefiting from its capabilities while safeguarding the human and ethical aspects of the sport. Coaches and players need to improve their digital literacy to fully leverage AI, understanding both its mechanics and its implications. Continued openness to learning and adapting will determine how effectively the tennis community can use AI tools.

Finally, collaboration with tech companies and academics can help establish benchmarks and best practices, ensuring that the integration of AI doesn't sideline the intrinsic thrill and human drama of tennis. Ongoing discussions about what AI means for sports in general, and tennis in particular, can help all stakeholders—players, coaches, fans, and technologists—navigate this transformative period more effectively.

Chapter 21:
AI in Tennis vs Other Sports

When comparing the impact of artificial intelligence across various sports, tennis presents a unique landscape where technology weaves seamlessly into the fabric of the game. While sports like football and basketball have leveraged AI primarily for tactical analytics and fan engagement, tennis stands out due to its embrace of real-time strategic insights and personalised training tools. In tennis, AI is not just enhancing performance but also reshaping the entire experience both on and off the court, from player preparation to post-match analysis. Other sports provide valuable lessons in AI integration, such as football's adoption of data analytics and individual player tracking, yet tennis uncovers unique challenges, like precision in shot mechanics, that AI directly addresses with cutting-edge solutions. Moreover, the opportunities for innovation in tennis are vast, as AI continually evolves to deliver intuitive training systems and smarter competition strategies, setting a benchmark for how technology can redefine an entire sport while ensuring its core essence remains intact.

Comparative Analysis

Artificial intelligence has found its way into numerous sports, each implementation bringing unique benefits and challenges. With tennis, AI's entry has been transformative, yet contrasting its role in other sports offers insightful perspectives on its potential scope and limitations. This comparative analysis uncovers the similarities and diversities in AI utilisation across sports, spotlighting the ways tennis can learn from or lead the charge in AI-driven innovation.

Football, or soccer to some, is perhaps the sport most comparable to tennis in terms of AI's impact, particularly in performance analytics. Football clubs have embraced AI to draw insights from vast datasets, influencing tactics and player management. However, the metric-based approach in football is often team-oriented. Tennis, being more individualised, requires AI to focus on personal attributes, such as the intricacies of player biomechanics or psychological states during matches. The real-time application in tennis, thus, becomes highly personalised, offering a nuanced edge when improving player performance.

In contrast, basketball has employed AI for player tracking and in-game strategy adjustments, often using wearable tech to gather data. While tennis has adopted wearables, its AI's focus extends into the broader realm of individual skill refinement and strategy prediction. The pace of AI-driven decision-making in basketball highlights a potential area for tennis to enhance its in-game analytical tools, allowing coaches and players to react swiftly to an opponent's shifting strategy.

Cricket's usage of AI leans heavily into fan engagement and broadcasting. Sydney cricket grounds, for instance, have used AI for real-time insight delivery to viewers, making matches far more interactive. Although tennis has begun to tap into these areas, the cricket model suggests a potential for even richer fan experiences. Tennis can augment this with content that's not only informative but also personal to each fan's viewing preference, perhaps using historical match data to deepen the narrative.

When it comes to injury prevention, American football offers significant lessons for tennis. The rigour of American football drives its adoption of AI for predicting and mitigating injuries, combining biomechanical data with AI algorithms to understand potential risk points. Tennis, with its repetitive motions and high physical stress conditions, stands to gain by adopting more advanced AI systems to pre-empt injuries, extending players' careers and ensuring optimum fitness.

In the realm of recruitment, sports like baseball have long employed data analytics, known as sabermetrics, to evaluate player potentials. AI's ability to analyse massive troves of data can help tennis enhance its scouting and recruitment efforts, identifying promising talent early on. Yet, tennis has the unique challenge of evaluating personal resilience and mental fortitude, areas where AI could be further refined to provide deeper insights into potential stars.

AI's treatment of game strategy in chess offers a fascinating parallel to tennis. Chess AI often involves evaluating millions of moves to craft championship-winning strategies. Tennis players and coaches can adopt similar predictive modelling methodologies to fine-tune match strategies, predicting opponents' shots or behavioural patterns. This level of complex decision-making, when translated into tennis, could significantly alter preparatory routines and match day tactics.

The ethical considerations around data privacy and AI are universally pressing across sports, yet tennis may face distinct challenges given the individual-focused nature of data collection. While basketball or football teams gather data at scale for squad dynamics, tennis zeroes in on player-specific metrics, amplifying privacy concerns. The sport could benefit from the frameworks developed in sports with similar concerns, adjusting them to fit its unique athlete-centric landscape.

Despite the varied implementations of AI across sports, tennis finds itself at a crossroads of opportunity and responsibility. By observing AI's role in other sports, tennis stakeholders can anticipate potential pitfalls and propel proactive advancements. As AI continues to advance, it's essential for tennis to harness this tool effectively, ensuring that enhancements do not overshadow the human artistry that is central to the sport's enduring appeal. Each learning point from other sports provides tennis with a gateway to not just match their successes but to forge a path where human talent and AI truly coalesce into extraordinary performances.

The ongoing dialogue within tennis about AI's place in the sport reflects broader industry trends. As AI becomes more integral, the potential to lead innovation while ensuring ethical integrity and accessibility remains crucial. Tennis has the chance to model a well-rounded, holistic approach to AI—one that other sports could follow. The future may yet reveal how tennis, by analysing and integrating AI insights from across the sporting world, will redefine the boundaries of individual and collective achievement, perhaps setting a new benchmark for AI in sports.

Lessons from Other Sports

Artificial intelligence has made waves in various sports, each offering unique lessons for its application in tennis. Sports such as football, basketball, and baseball have long embraced AI, revealing insights into analytics, coaching, and fan engagement that tennis can learn from. By examining how AI has transformed these sports, we can glean strategies to enhance the tennis experience.

Football, with its grand stage and global following, serves as a prime example of AI's transformative power. Predictive analytics in football have revolutionised player scouting, match strategy, and injury prevention. By analysing thousands of data points, AI systems forecast player performance and team dynamics, making recruitment more strategic. Tennis can learn from the depth of analytical insight football achieves, particularly in player development and match preparation.

Basketball has embraced AI for its real-time analytics and player performance evaluation. Systems track every movement on the court, providing granular data that informs tactical decisions. This level of detail, if applied to tennis, could support real-time coaching interventions and strategic adjustments mid-match. Tennis could leverage similar technologies to monitor player positioning and shot selection, leading to more dynamic coaching methods.

Baseball, often hailed for its early adoption of statistics, shows how deeply AI can embed itself into the fabric of a sport. The use of AI in baseball extends from sabermetrics to predictive modelling for game outcomes. The sport illustrates the power of data-driven strategies that could significantly enhance tennis coaching and player performance analysis. Tennis might emulate baseball by adopting complex analytical models to determine match strategies and player matchups.

In addition, the use of wearables and biometric tracking in American football has provided insights into player health and performance optimisation. Tracking physiological data helps mitigate injury risks while enhancing training regimes. Tennis players, too, could benefit from this type of wearable technology, allowing for personalised training plans and injury prevention strategies based on real-time data.

Rugby, a sport characterised by its physical intensity, offers lessons in AI's role in injury management and prevention. By leveraging machine learning algorithms, rugby teams predict potential injuries, thus reducing the physical toll on players. This approach aligns seamlessly with tennis's need to maintain player health and longevity, especially in a sport where injuries significantly impact careers.

Cycling's use of AI showcases how biometric data can be maximised for endurance sports. Cyclists employ AI to optimise training load, nutrition, and race strategies based on physiological feedback. Tennis can assimilate these techniques to enhance player stamina and performance sustainability, crucial given the sport's demanding nature.

Cricket, with its detailed player and match data, has utilised AI to simulate game scenarios and predict outcomes. This predictive modelling informs strategies and player roles within matches. Tennis, although a more individual-centric sport, could adopt similar simulations to pre-emptively strategise for diverse playing styles and conditions, improving player adaptability.

In motorsports, AI has revolutionised car performance and racing strategy. Real-time data collection during races leads to split-second adjustments that can mean the difference between victory and defeat. The concept of dynamic, real-time analysis could be carried over to tennis, where match conditions, player focus, and fatigue levels are continuously changing.

eSports, a rapidly growing industry, highlights the potential of AI in enhancing fan engagement through interactive platforms and personalised content. Here lies a significant takeaway for tennis organisations seeking to deepen their connection with audiences. By employing AI to create tailored viewer experiences, tennis has the potential to broaden its appeal and accessibility.

Despite these advancements, each sport faces unique challenges with AI integration, such as data privacy and ethical concerns. Football's experience with fan data privacy, for instance, could serve as a cautionary tale for tennis as it ventures further into AI-led innovations. Balancing technological advances with ethical considerations remains a crucial lesson across the board.

Another challenge is the economic barrier to AI technology. Sports such as basketball and baseball have high entry costs for advanced analytical tools, which could also impact tennis. Lessons from basketball show the importance of finding cost-effective solutions, ensuring AI's benefits reach all levels of the sport, from amateur to professional.

Tennis can learn from the collaborative efforts seen in other sports, where partnerships between tech companies and sporting bodies have spurred innovation. Joint ventures foster research and development, leading to groundbreaking technologies. Tennis should nurture similar collaborations to stay at the forefront of AI advancements.

In conclusion, the integration of AI in other sports provides a roadmap for tennis. The ability to adapt insights from various disciplines while addressing tennis's unique needs offers an exciting future. The lessons from football's detailed analytics, basketball's real-time strategy adjustments, and baseball's predictive models all provide rich inspiration. As tennis continues its AI journey, embracing these cross-sport lessons will only enhance its appeal and competitive edge.

Unique Challenges and Opportunities

Artificial intelligence has carved its niche within the sporting world, offering a range of advancements across many disciplines. However, when we compare tennis to other sports, we uncover unique challenges and opportunities that distinguish tennis as a prime candidate for AI intervention. While all sports can leverage data for improved performance, tennis' individual nature and global reach provide a distinct landscape for AI innovation.

One of the significant challenges in integrating AI into tennis lies in its inherently individualistic nature. Unlike team sports such as football or basketball, where strategies involve the coordination of multiple players, tennis demands an intense focus on individuality. Players often rely on personalised strategies that can dramatically shift based on their strengths and weaknesses. This necessitates a more focussed and bespoke AI application capable of analysing idiosyncratic player behaviours and preferences. Personalisation is not merely a luxury but a necessity here, as AI systems need to adapt rapidly to the on-court dynamism unique to each match and player.

Another challenge arises from the variability of playing conditions. Tennis is played on diverse surfaces each influencing the game's pace, bounce, and strategy. AI must account for these variable conditions when generating predictive models or crafting player-specific training regimens. In cricket or baseball, for example, an AI system might focus primarily on player stats or weather conditions, but tennis demands a broader focus. Grass, clay, and hard courts each introduce distinct challenges that AI must navigate effectively, adapting its analysis to accommodate different levels of friction, speed, and air resistance.

Opportunities, too, are abundant. Tennis offers a treasure trove of data-rich scenarios where AI can shine. The sport's history of extensive data capture—from scores to serve speeds to unforced errors—lays the groundwork for AI optimisation. The opportunity to refine predictive models based on existing data is immense. Teams can unlock nuanced insights into opponent strategies, develop tailored training plans, and carve out new performance metrics.

Moreover, AI can drastically revolutionise fan engagement within tennis, creating innovative ways for spectators to connect with the sport. Football and basketball have already set precedents with AI-aided virtual realities and interactive platforms. Still, tennis provides a fresh canvas for experimentation. With AI, fans could delve deeper into analysis, understanding match statistics with the same complexity as players and coaches. For instance, AI could personalise broadcasts, offering stats-based predictions or highlighting different player performance metrics based on fan interest.

In the realm of ethics and fairness, tennis faces unique challenges distinct from those in team sports. The precision required in line calling and the subjectivity in judging have historically sparked controversies. While sports like football have adopted technologies such as the VAR system to assist in decision-making, tennis must incorporate AI in ways that uphold integrity without overshadowing the human element. The automation of line calls through AI promises accuracy but needs widespread acceptance among players and officials alike.

The opportunities for grassroots development present another compelling facet. Tennis, compared to sports with more extensive global reach, often deals with disparities in access and resources; AI technology offers solutions to bridge these gaps. Smart coaching tools powered by AI can democratise elite-level training, bringing insights once reserved for top-tier athletes to amateur levels. Such technology could identify talent in undeveloped regions, broadening tennis' reach and inclusivity.

Additionally, AI offers invaluable opportunities in coaching and training optimisation. Tennis coaches can leverage AI to enhance decision-making, providing real-time feedback and personalised training recommendations. Unlike sports with extensive squad strategies, tennis coaching can focus intensely on player-specific analytics. The harnessing of AI here can lead to groundbreaking advances in player development, with coaches crafting hyper-personalised regimens that cater directly to individual needs, whether physical, strategic, or psychological.

Injury prevention in tennis embodies both a challenge and an opportunity for AI. Due to the repetitive nature of strokes and constant movement demands, tennis players often face overuse injuries. AI-driven wearable technologies can monitor players' biomechanics and workload, offering real-time data to prevent injuries before they occur. By comparing tennis-specific data to what AI is achieving in sports like athletics or cycling, better insights into training loads and recovery profiles can be extracted.

From a broadcasting perspective, the challenge lies in maintaining the human essence amidst increased AI utilisation for automating highlights or providing live commentary. While other sports have adopted AI commentators, tennis enthusiasts hold strong connections to the traditional auditory experiences of the game. Navigating this balance without alienating fans, while simultaneously enriching the viewing experience, remains a vital task.

Finally, across these challenges lies an underpinning opportunity for collaboration between AI developers and tennis professionals to craft solutions specifically attuned to the sport's nuances. The hybrid of a global game, admired for both its simplicities and complexities, invites an AI evolution that respects tradition while embracing innovation. This collaborative effort can further push the boundaries of what AI can do within tennis, transforming it from a reactive to a proactive, visionary tool.

As AI continues to mature in its deployment, the distinct pathways within tennis will likely serve as a blueprint for other individual sports. The game will continue to pose unique challenges, from ethical considerations to personalisation demands, yet the accompanying opportunities for growth and enhancement remain robust and abundant. It is within this dynamic interplay of challenge and opportunity that the future of AI in tennis will truly be written.

Chapter 22:
Player Perspectives on AI

In the world of elite tennis, where every nuance can change the game's outcome, players are increasingly vocal about the role AI plays in refining their performance and strategies. Many top players marvel at AI-powered tools that bring unprecedented precision to shot analysis and tactical preparation. Some share anecdotes of how AI has allowed them to identify and rectify flaws they had never noticed before, adding a layer of depth to their understanding of their own gameplay. However, the embrace of AI is not universal; a few express concerns about the possible erosion of the sport's human elements, worried that over-reliance on technology might dilute the instincts and artistry that define tennis. These insights form a fascinating tapestry of opinions, illustrating that while AI holds the promise of revolutionising training regimes and match preparations, the heart of tennis still beats strongest in its human participants.

Interviews with Professional Players

In the labyrinth of backhands, forehands, and strategic mind games, tennis has quietly ushered in a technological ally—artificial intelligence. As we navigate the shifting landscape of this sport, hearing from those on the front lines offers unparalleled insight. Professional players have unique perspectives on AI's role, each with their interpretations, apprehensions, and aspirations. Let's delve into these interviews, varying in tone from enthusiastic to contemplative, highlighting both AI's potential and perceived threats to tradition.

Consider, for example, a seasoned player who has witnessed the sport's evolution first-hand, from wooden rackets to high-tech composites. This player reminisces about days spent practising without today's digital assistants, offering an unvarnished glimpse into how far we've come. Now, with AI-driven insights, they can dissect game footage with precision, identifying nuances and inefficiencies barely noticeable through the naked eye. "It's like having a coach that sees beyond human capability," they might say, capturing AI's essence in training sessions.

Yet not all players meet AI with open arms. Some express a sort of quiet unease, fearing that the game they love might pivot too sharply away from its core. The tactile feel of sweat and grit doesn't quite translate through a digital lens. One player expressed concern over becoming overly reliant on data, worrying it might erode their intuitive game sense that years on the court have honed. "AI offers a brain, but what about the heart?" This sentiment echoes throughout the locker rooms and press conferences, a reminder that even as technology advances, the game's soulful artistry remains sacrosanct to its purveyors.

Other athletes see AI as a levelling field, a chance for those outside the elite strata to elevate their game. A young, emerging player shared their experiences with AI as a transformative force, akin to having a personalised playbook crafted from the strategies of legends. Through AI, they could bridge experience gaps and compete with veterans of the sport, making previously insurmountable challenges just a bit more conquerable. "AI gives us that fighting chance," they argue, underscoring the democratising potential of technology in sport.

Discussing the tangible benefits AI brings, several players note changes in how injuries are managed. By leveraging AI analytics, a player is better equipped to understand their body's limitations and capabilities. One athlete detailed their journey back to form post-injury, crediting AI for predictive analytics that tailored their regimen to avoid overstraining, thus preventing further setbacks. "It was like having a guardian angel guiding every step," they offered, a testament to AI's burgeoning role in elongating athletic careers.

Moreover, technology-savvy players relish the fusion of human strategy with algorithmic precision, emphasising the role of AI in enhancing match strategies. With AI, the collaborative process between player and coach transforms significantly. Matches are no longer brute contests of endurance alone but intellectual battles orchestrated with the aid of data-driven strategies. "It's chess on the court," proclaimed one Grand Slam champion, illustrating the seismic shift AI catalyzes in strategic acumen.

However, AI's integration isn't without its learning curve. Players sometimes find themselves at a crossroads, navigating AI's intricate inputs and their own instincts. The sheer volume of data can drown out a player's natural rhythms, making intuitive play more challenging. Some recount experiences where following AI-suggested strategies conflicted with instinctual decisions on the court, providing fodder for reflection on AI's limitations. "Finding balance is key," one player candidly observed, capturing the dance between analytics and flair.

Though these voices vary, a recurring theme emerges: the fusion of tradition and technology. For many, AI represents not a replacement but an enhancement. It augments training and planning but never seeks to supersede the essence of tennis. Echoing across these interviews, players advocate for AI as a co-pilot, steering but not taking the helm outright.

Professional players champion collaboration, suggesting that AI fosters a sense of shared advancement. By pooling experiences and feedback, they propose a reciprocal relationship—AI enhances their game, and they, in turn, refine AI's capabilities through practical application. Players see themselves as architects in this digital age, engaged in a symbiotic dialogue with technology.

Ultimately, the insights from these interviews highlight a collective desire to respect the game's legacy while embracing tech-driven innovation. AI doesn't merely spectate from the sidelines; it actively participates in the modern iteration of tennis, creating a living, breathing tapestry woven from past, present, and future threads. As these players continue to write their narratives, the dialogue surrounding AI's role promises to enrich the sport, inviting both sceptics and believers to ponder the infinite possibilities ahead.

Their stories leave us to contemplate not just what AI can do for tennis players, but what players can teach AI. As they stride onto the court, rackets in hand and algorithms at their fingertips, they embody the resilience and adaptability at the heart of sport itself—a true testament to a remarkable synergy between human ingenuity and technological prowess.

Personal Anecdotes

In the often exhilarating but solitary world of elite tennis, players find themselves navigating a unique intersection where the rigour of physical competition meets the burgeoning landscape of artificial intelligence. While AI promises a revolution that transforms playing strategies and performance analytics, its real impact is perhaps best understood through the voices on the court—the players themselves. Their stories become windows into a world adapting to the accelerating changes brought by AI.

Consider Emma, a rising star on the circuit from Brighton. She recalled the initial trepidation she felt when AI-enhanced analytics were first introduced into her training sessions. For Emma, like many players, tennis had always been a sport of instinct and muscle memory.

However, the AI program suggested slight modifications to her forehand technique, proposing nuances she hadn't considered. Over time, she embraced incorporating these technological insights and credited them for fine-tuning the precision of her shots—a critical edge in an otherwise close match last season. "It was like having another coach," she said, "one that could see angles and patterns that I couldn't." Her story reflects a common theme where technology complements, rather than overtakes, the traditional coaching wisdom.

Then there's the account of Liam, a seasoned player based in Edinburgh, who viewed AI with a mix of scepticism and awe. He shared a particular anecdote that sticks with him to this day. "During a training match, the AI analysed our rally and predicted shots with such accuracy that it almost felt eerie. It pointed out a subtle tendency I had of favouring my backhand during high-pressure points," Liam said with a chuckle. "You know, sometimes I think it knows me better than I know myself. But it's not always right, that's for sure." In Liam's narrative, AI emerges not as an infallible oracle but as a tool—remarkably effective yet occasionally limited by the unpredictabilities of human effort and resolve.

Not all experiences with AI have been embraced so warmly. Take the case of Sarah, a middle-ranked professional who juggled her competitive career with online university courses in computer science. Despite her tech-savvy background, Sarah initially found herself mystified and somewhat frustrated. Whenever the AI system recommended alterations in her serve, Sarah's natural instinct was to question its validity. However, a turning point came during a practice session captured on video—and subsequently analysed by AI. She realised the system had been correctly pinpointing her tendency to rush the toss, thus affecting her timing. "It was like seeing the game from a fresh perspective," Sarah admitted. "It revolutionised how I prepare and counter opponents." Her story exemplifies the paradigm shift where even knowledgeable players must reinvent their self-perception in response to technology.

In contrast, Jake's journey with AI paints a picture of seamless integration. A junior player from Manchester with aspirations to join the professional ranks, Jake grew up in an era where digital augmentation was almost a given. He recalled how his smart racket, laden with sensors, became an invaluable partner. "I was able to pick up patterns in my play that I never would have noticed otherwise," he enthused. Jake's AI-enabled training transformed his technique and gameplay approach even at such an early stage in his career. His tale illustrates a new wave of athletes who instinctively meld human skill with digital enhancements from the very onset of their sporting journeys, embracing AI as a natural ally.

It's perhaps telling that the diversity in anecdotes echoes the broader theme of AI's role—not as an imposing entity that dictates the terms of a player's journey, but as an addition to their toolkit, offering insights and innovations. The personal experiences of players highlight a broader acceptance, yet candid caution, that technology is an enabler, not an oracle. While AI may not hold all the answers, its capacity to offer unprecedented insights means a future where players who harmonise their instincts with intelligent inputs will likely have the upper hand.

Even beyond the practical implications, tales like those of Emma, Liam, Sarah, and Jake reveal the quintessential tennis characteristics persisting in this new era—resilience, adaptability, and the pursuit of excellence. The way these athletes have begun to engage AI narrates a story of evolution that mirrors tennis' historical transitions, from wooden to composite rackets or from outdated techniques to cutting-edge strategies. Each anecdote, laden with personal insights and revelations, serves to illuminate not just the individual paths each player takes but also their reflections on the sport they love—and its confluence with technology.

Looking ahead, these first-hand experiences hint at potential shifts in tennis culture, where AI guidance becomes increasingly ubiquitous and perhaps indispensable. As these athletes demonstrate, embracing AI is not about replacing traditional methods but enriching them, underscoring a trend that treats technology as an intimate partner in the relentless quest for improvement. Such personal narratives signal an exciting horizon for tennis—a future shaped by technological brilliance through the eyes of those who know the game best.

The way forwards seems planted at a crossroad of curiosity and nostalgia, much like the narratives of these players. Their stories form a collective tapestry that speaks to the wider landscape of AI's transformative impact on tennis, as the sport prepares to tread even further along its innovative path. These anecdotes provide not only a lens into how today's professionals are navigating change but also a beacon illuminating the possibilities for those yet to lace up their shoes and step onto the court of tomorrow.

The Human Element in AI

In the fast-paced world of tennis today, artificial intelligence isn't just a tool; it's a partner in the game. As AI systems weave themselves intricately into the fabric of tennis, it's imperative to highlight the symbiosis between humans and technology. Tennis players find themselves at a crucial intersection where human intuition meets AI's computational power. Indeed, the interplay of these elements raises a compelling question: how do players maintain their identity and creativity when data-driven insights hold such sway?

Despite AI's obvious advantages in analyzing performance and suggesting strategic improvements, the irreplaceable human touch imbues the game with its essence. A player's style, developed over years of practice and reflective of personality and intuition, remains a uniquely human attribute. There's no algorithm for the thrill of a last-minute comeback or the instinctive choice of a risky shot that pays off. AI can suggest optimal shot selections based on data, but instincts developed through experience play a significant role when the moment arrives.

The balance of trust between a player and AI is a fascinating dance. On one hand, there's data; cold, calculated, and emotionally detached. On the other, there's intuition; the spiritual and most visceral of human traits. Serena Williams' fierce competitiveness or Roger Federer's effortless grace can't be reduced to mere numbers. Yet, these players might also rely on AI's analyses to refine tactics or understand opponents better. Trusting in AI's guidance enhances, rather than diminishes, their humanity on the court.

These days, coaches often act as interpreters, mediating between the flow of statistics and the athlete's natural flair. A coach's skill isn't just in strategising based on data but using data to empower and embolden their players. Coaches inspire athletes to believe in themselves, nurturing the emotional and psychological facets that AI simply can't replicate. They transform data into meaningful insights, resulting in more informed decisions without undermining the player's confidence or smothering creative spontaneity.

Moreover, AI's role doesn't stop at the boundary lines of the court. It extends into mental conditioning, emotional health, and therapeutic approaches, enhancing training experiences and personal well-being. By quantifying stress levels or predicting mental breakdown, AI aids emotional resilience. Yet, it's the human touch that provides empathy, understanding, and motivation, turning an athlete's weaknesses into strengths. This blend of tech and human insight marks the new era of tennis as a holistic journey.

Looking through a player's perspective, AI offers a mirror reflecting back the nuances of their actions and providing unprecedented awareness of their performance rhythms. This awareness, however, is double-edged. While it can illuminate paths to improvement, it can also intimidate and overwhelm players with its sheer precision and unemotional output. It takes human wisdom and mentoring to manage this potential overload, ensuring that analytics remain empowering rather than discouraging.

As AI sheds light on aspects of performance previously hidden in shadows, the question arises: does it risk stripping away the mystery that makes tennis so engaging in the first place? For some players, relying too heavily on algorithms might make each movement and decision feel predetermined, lacking the suspense and drama intrinsic to the sport. Yet it's important to remember that AI's role is to complement rather than supplant human ingenuity.

The harmony of AI working alongside human creativity can cultivate potential in ways previously unimaginable. Innovative players like Novak Djokovic and Bianca Andreescu have embraced AI as a cornerstone of training regime optimisations, demonstrating that embracing technology doesn't equate to losing touch with the game's human elements. Their approach underscores an acceptance of AI as an ally, harnessing its strengths while maintaining control over its implementation.

Moreover, players must navigate the moral and ethical considerations AI's involvement brings to the forefront. Being aware of data privacy and intellectual property concerns, they must ponder the extent and nature of AI's role in their sport. This awareness reflects a broader, more conscientious engagement with technology that's thoughtful and responsible, shaping a sustainable future for AI in tennis.

Ultimately, AI and human intuition in tennis coalesce to evoke a richer, more dynamic approach to the sport. This partnership encourages tennis to push traditional boundaries, venturing into novel realms of possibility while respecting the game's core spirit. As AI technology continues to evolve and integrate within tennis, it will never supplant the intuition, feel, and spontaneity that the human element brings. Rather, it will cultivate a symbiosis where the most human emotions of joy, triumph, and perseverance continue to take centre stage, driven and amplified by the AI frameworks quietly operating behind the scenes.

By embracing this transformative journey, players are not merely spectators to their own evolution but active participants, shaping the future of tennis with each match. AI, in its place, amplifies their potential, yet stands aside as the athlete themselves, fuelled by passion and heart, etches their narrative onto the court. This evolving partnership between player and AI promises a future where art and data dance in tandem, adding new dimensions to the story of tennis.

Chapter 23:
AI as a Coach's Ally

AI has emerged as a transformative force in the world of tennis coaching, acting as a powerful ally that enhances both training efficiency and strategic play. By providing real-time feedback, AI systems allow coaches to gain unprecedented insights into a player's performance. This technology doesn't replace the time-honoured intuition a coach brings to the game; rather, it augments their capabilities, offering detailed analyses that were once impossible to achieve so quickly. Through AI, coaches can swiftly identify areas for improvement, tailor sessions to a player's unique needs, and observe patterns in play that inform more effective strategies. Success stories abound, illustrating how AI brings an array of benefits to the training environment. By combining traditional wisdom with cutting-edge technology, AI is redefining what coaches can achieve, encouraging exciting and dynamic developments in their methodologies.

Enhancing Training Sessions

Training sessions in tennis have traditionally relied on the keen eyes of coaches, the repetitive practices of drills, and the lessons drawn from match performances. However, with the advent of artificial intelligence, the realm of training is experiencing transformative innovations. AI has stepped in not just as an analytical observer, but as an active participant, empowering coaches and players with precise insights that are reshaping the training landscape.

One of the key ways AI enhances training is through its ability to process vast amounts of data in real time. AI-powered systems can analyse a player's performance minute by minute, breaking down each movement, shot, and decision into actionable data. This data is then converted into insights that help structure personalised training sessions tailored to a player's strengths and weaknesses. Instead of generic drills, players can engage in focused practice that targets specific areas of improvement, ensuring that the efforts put into training sessions lead to tangible progress.

Smart rackets are at the forefront of this AI-driven training revolution. Equipped with sensors and connectivity features, these rackets capture detailed data on each stroke—a speed, spin, angle of contact, and more. The feedback from these rackets, when integrated with AI analytics, offers players immediate performance indicators, facilitating an understanding of not just what needs correction, but why. This real-time feedback promotes quicker adjustments, allowing players to refine their techniques on the go, ultimately optimizing their practice efficiency.

Furthermore, advanced video analysis tools powered by AI cater to enhancing strategic aspects of the game. These tools can dissect past match footage to study opponents' tendencies and predict potential strategies. For a player, this means entering a match equipped with a comprehensive playbook anchored on data-driven assumptions. During training, players can simulate these strategies, gaining confidence and preparedness, enhancing their decision-making process under pressure conditions.

Personalised training programs are another remarkable innovation brought by AI. These programs adapt to a player's involvement and growth, dynamically restructuring based on improved metrics or newly identified areas needing attention. The adaptability of such programs ensures that players are not stuck in monotonous routines but are continuously evolving. Coaches can use these insights to monitor performance trends over time, giving them the ability to make informed decisions about workload management, recovery planning, and long-term development goals.

Moreover, AI assists in injury prevention through predictive analytics. By tracking biometric data through wearables, AI systems can notice deviations that may signal potential injury risks, allowing for preemptive interventions. During training sessions, these insights inform coaches about when to intensify exercises or when to dial them back, ensuring players maintain peak physical condition without overstraining.

Integrating AI in training not only aids in refining technical skills but also supports mental conditioning. AI offers psychological metrics derived from analysing behaviour patterns, offering actionable insights into a player's mental state over time. With these insights, coaches can tailor mental resilience exercises within training regimens, boosting a player's cognitive competitiveness, focus, and stress management.

The collaborative relationship between AI and coaching lays the groundwork for a future where training sessions become both scientific and inspirational. Coaches no longer rely solely on intuition but have a cohort of data-backed insights that boost their coaching efficacy. For players, this symbiotic partnership provides a dual advantage: honing their physical skills while nurturing the mental fortitude required for high-stakes matches.

However, embedding AI into training does not dilute the personal touch of traditional coaching; instead, it enhances it. Coaches can focus more on motivational aspects and strategy, knowing that the tedious task of data collection and analysis is handled by intelligent systems. The result is a harmony where personal intuition meets cutting-edge technology, leading to unprecedented levels of player development.

As AI continues to evolve, the potential applications in tennis training sessions seem limitless. The ability to simulate match conditions using AI-driven virtual environments could be the next leap forward, providing players with immersive experiences that prepare them for various competitive situations. Leveraging AI for tactical adjustments during practice could create a dynamic learning environment where players are constantly adapting and improving.

The effectiveness of these AI tools in training reinforces the need for clear communication between technology and humans. Coaches and players must collaborate closely to interpret AI-generated data accurately and use it to inform decisions. Training sessions of the future will likely exist as interactive dialogues between AI systems, coaches, and players, creating a rich, participatory environment focused on continuous growth and achievement.

The evolution of AI in enhancing tennis training sessions highlights the revolutionary changes on the horizon for the sport. As technological advancements continue to integrate seamlessly with human expertise, the potential for unparalleled improvements in player performance and coaching strategies becomes evident. In this unfolding narrative, artificial intelligence acts not just as a tool but as an invaluable ally in the ascent to mastery on the tennis courts.

Real-Time Feedback

The modern tennis court is more than just lines and nets; it's now a digital playground brimming with opportunities for instantaneous insights. As artificial intelligence reshapes the sporting landscape, its capacity to provide real-time feedback is revolutionising the coach-player dynamic. Gone are the days where feedback was limited to a coach's manual observations during play. AI now empowers coaches with immediate, precise data that can be used to adjust strategies and enhance player performance on the fly.

Real-time feedback powered by AI enables coaches to make informed adjustments in the midst of matches. Consider a scenario where a player struggles with their serve during a critical match. AI tools can quickly analyse factors like serve speed, angle, and spin, providing a detailed breakdown. The coach, equipped with this data, suggests minor tweaks that help the player re-align their serve, potentially altering the course of the match. This capability to make data-informed decisions instantaneously is a game-changer.

At the heart of real-time feedback is the capability of AI to process massive datasets at a remarkable speed. Advanced algorithms can sift through historical match data, live performance metrics, and even biomechanical analyses. By comparing this information against optimal performance parameters, AI systems can deliver precise feedback in a matter of seconds. This immediacy not only enhances the tactical aspect of the game but also significantly boosts a player's confidence knowing they have scientifically-backed guidance on hand.

Beyond strategic adjustments, AI-driven feedback offers insights into a player's physical condition during play. Using data from wearable technologies, AI can track biometric signals such as heart rate, hydration levels, and muscle exertion. Coaches can monitor these parameters in real-time, allowing them to preemptively address potential fatigue, cramps, or other health concerns before they become critical issues. This level of monitoring ensures that players operate within safe physical limits, reducing injury risks and promoting longevity in their careers.

Furthermore, real-time feedback isn't solely confined to physical attributes; it also covers psychological aspects. Modern AI systems can detect subtleties in a player's body language and behaviour, providing insights into their mental state. By analysing facial expressions, posture, and reaction times, AI offers coaches additional layers of information that are difficult to discern through human observation alone. This psychological dimension enhances holistic player development and supports mental resilience, which is as crucial as physical prowess on the court.

Moreover, AI's capability to offer real-time feedback fosters greater collaboration between teams. For example, broadcasters can leverage this technology to engage audiences by providing real-time stats and analysis, enriching the viewing experience. Similarly, players can access this data through smart devices, receiving direct guidance during practice sessions or matches, further encouraging a cohesive team environment and shared goals.

It must be noted, however, that the human element in coaching remains indispensable. AI's role is to augment human expertise, not replace it. The depth of insights a seasoned coach can draw from AI-generated data enriches the coaching dialogue. By blending intuitive expertise with precise technological input, coaches enhance their player's skill set more effectively than ever before. This symbiotic relationship between coach and technology is where the true potential of AI is realised.

Recognising the potential of AI-driven real-time feedback, tennis organisations and institutions are increasingly making this technology accessible. From elite academies to grassroots initiatives, the deployment of cost-effective AI solutions is democratising access to advanced coaching tools. Young players and amateurs can now benefit from the same level of insights previously reserved for professional athletes, levelling the playing field and fostering future talent.

As tennis continues to evolve at the intersection of traditional wisdom and cutting-edge technology, real-time feedback exemplifies the transformative power of AI. It's not merely about keeping pace with the modern game but redefining the metrics of success. Coaches who embrace these advancements find themselves well-equipped to cultivate the next generation of champions, armed with an integrated approach that respects the game's history while boldly venturing into its future.

In essence, AI's role in delivering real-time feedback enriches all facets of tennis coaching. Whether it's making split-second decisions in high-stakes matches, ensuring player well-being, or enhancing the subtle mental aspects of the game, the advantages are both profound and widespread. As AI technology progresses, its ability to further refine and enhance real-time feedback will no doubt solidify its place as an invaluable ally for coaches around the world. However, as these technologies develop, maintaining a focus on ethical deployment and privacy will be vital to sustaining trust and integrity within this burgeoning field.

Success Narratives

In an era where technology finds its stronghold in sports, tennis has emerged as a fertile ground for artificial intelligence to demonstrate its transformative potential. Stories of success abound, as AI relentlessly pushes the boundaries of what athletes, coaches, and even fans deem possible. The synthesis of human ingenuity and machine precision has led to remarkable narratives that inspire and motivate both budding and seasoned tennis players alike. Let's explore some of these compelling tales where AI has played an indispensable role in shaping triumph.

One of the resounding success narratives comes from a young tennis player, Samantha Carter, a rising star on the junior circuit. Struggling with consistency in her backhand, Samantha turned to AI-powered training tools to address this Achilles' heel. Utilising advanced video analysis, her coach dissected each stroke, drawing on AI to identify subtle patterns and minute errors imperceptible to the human eye. The feedback was instantaneous. Every time Samantha swung her racket, she received real-time adjustments, transforming her weakness into a formidable strength. Within months, the results were evident on the scoreboard, as she began winning matches that once slipped from her grasp.

Equally inspiring is the story of Martin Lee, a seasoned coach known for his traditional approach. Initially sceptical about integrating AI into coaching, Martin decided to experiment with data-driven methodologies for an upcoming tournament with a high-stakes player. Leveraging predictive modelling and shot selection algorithms, he devised strategies that seemed nearly clairvoyant. As matches progressed, Martin's coaching strategies shifted seamlessly in response to the AI-generated insights, adapting to the opponent's ever-changing tactics. His player advanced further than ever in the competition, culminating in a decisive victory that silenced countless critics.

Casual observers might wonder about the human element amidst all this technology. However, AI isn't replacing the human touch; it's enhancing it. This is evident in how players like Rafael Gomez have integrated biometric tracking and stress management tools, fundamentally altering their mental conditioning. Once plagued by nerves on the court, Rafael began using AI-driven psychological metrics, which revealed a pattern of mental fatigue that correlated with match times. Adjusting training schedules and employing AI-derived relaxation techniques, Rafael transformed nervous energy into laser-like focus. His improved mental resilience didn't just impact his game; it became a pivotal narrative in his journey towards resilience and mastery.

Then there's the case of elite clubs incorporating AI into their scouting and recruitment processes. Stories surface of coaches discovering players in seemingly unexpected locales, thanks to AI's ability to sift through countless matches across global tournaments. One such narrative highlights the discovery of an Australian player, unseen by scouts but identified by an AI-driven analysis of match statistics and playing style. This young talent was given an opportunity she might have otherwise missed, altering her career trajectory dramatically.

Success stories aren't just tethered to individual performances or coaching breakthroughs. On a grander scale, entire organisations have transformed their operational models with AI, witnessing unprecedented efficiencies. Tournament organisers employing AI for intelligent infrastructure management have seen significant improvements in managing logistics and fan engagement. Automating line calls with precision previously unachievable by human adjudicators, these systems ensured fairness and heightened trust among players, resulting in highly competitive play.

Infrastructure isn't merely about systems and efficiency; it's about creating a seamless experience where every participant feels engaged. AI-driven platforms have enabled real-time interactions with fans, offering personalised content that keeps the sport dynamic and alive. This shift has led to an increased fan base, as people connect in ways that were unimaginable before the AI wave. For instance, fans can now receive tailored content that matches their preferences, aligning with teams and players in more meaningful and exciting ways.

The fusion of AI in tennis has also provided unparalleled insights during injury recovery processes. Athletes recovering from injuries often form part of these compelling success narratives. A vivid story is that of Caroline White, who faced a career-threatening wrist injury. Traditionally daunting, the recovery was accelerated by AI's predictive models and real-time health monitoring. Through tailored rehabilitation programs, monitored closely by AI, Caroline returned to the game quicker than any conventional method could permit, not only regaining her form but reaching new athletic heights.

Perhaps the most admirable success narratives are those shaped by AI that thrive not just at the elite level, but permeate down to grassroots tennis. Schools and community clubs adopting AI-powered technologies report significant athlete development, providing access and insights previously limited to the professional echelons. These narratives echo a democratisation of tennis knowledge, illustrating the transformative potential AI holds for every level of sport.

These success narratives collectively reveal a sport in symbiosis with technology, where AI assists in maximising potential, optimising strategies, and even nurturing dreams. They're testimonies not just to the capabilities of AI, but to human aspiration and resilience, depicting a vibrant future for tennis that reaches beyond mere technology, into realms of unparalleled human achievement and connection. As AI continues to evolve, the success narratives within tennis will only grow richer, offering endless possibilities for players and coaches eager to harness its power for their personal journeys and goals.

Chapter 24:
Crowd-Sourced Intelligence

In the realm of artificial intelligence and tennis, the rise of crowd-sourced intelligence marks an intriguing development where the immense potential of collective human effort and AI converge. Imagine an ecosystem where the intuitive observations of fans and nuanced insights from players feed into dynamic AI systems, creating a vibrant tapestry of shared knowledge. Open data initiatives play a pivotal role here, allowing enthusiasts and experts alike to contribute valuable in-game analytics and performance metrics. This democratisation of information fosters a community-driven innovation cycle, enhancing the sport's strategic fabric with a diverse range of perspectives. Such collaborative intelligence not only refines AI algorithms but also propels tennis into a new era where the sport evolves by harnessing the collective brainpower of its global community. The implications for enhancing player performance and enriching the fan experience are vast, making tennis not just a game played on courts, but a continuously evolving narrative shaped by a networked collective of minds.

Fan and Player Inputs

The nature of tennis is changing dynamically, fuelled by the collective voice of fans and players. This transformation is deeply tied to the synergy between artificial intelligence and the insights gathered from those who live and breathe the sport. Their voices, now more amplified through AI technologies, offer a trove of data that influences decisions on and off the court. Today, AI systems are designed not just to process data, but to understand tennis audiences more intimately. These varied inputs pull from across the spectrum of play and fandom, creating an eco-system of crowd-sourced intelligence.

For the die-hard fan in the stands, every match presents an opportunity to contribute deeper insights into the game. Data collected from social media platforms, fan forums, and interactive polls are fed into AI models that analyse sentiment and predict trends. These collective opinions can highlight emerging talents, spotlight sensational matches, or even campaign for rule changes. AI employs natural language processing to sift through vast amounts of unstructured data, extracting meaningful insights that resonate throughout the tennis world.

Players, too, provide a rich stream of data, feeding this intelligence network that tennis has become. Inputs from wearables that track biometrics, alongside player feedback, form a crucial part of this lattice. Players have started engaging directly with AI platforms during training sessions, offering real-time inputs that help refine AI algorithms and, in turn, their performance. The symbiotic relationship means that player feedback continuously optimises the AI systems, aiding in perfecting shot accuracy or resilience strategies during high-pressure points.

The accessibility of input channels has exploded, owing to advances in technology that allow fans and players to communicate with the sport's governing bodies and tech entities seamlessly. Whether it's through apps that allow users to commentate on a live match or through sophisticated AI interfaces that integrate fan predictions, the barriers have diminished significantly. These crowd-sourced perspectives are shaping everything from scheduling matches to reconsidering tournament formats, utilising AI to weigh popular demand against logistical and commercial constraints.

In enhancing player inputs, AI technologies often employ methods like feedback loops, where insights from athletes directly refine AI systems. This approach ranges from tweaking hardware, like smart rackets, to adjusting solo training sessions according to a player's physiological and mental condition. Players not only become consumers of this crowd-sourced intelligence but also key contributors. This dual role evolves AI systems into tools that understand and anticipate transitions in player form and needs, sculpting training regimes to be more effective and personalised.

The interplay between AI, fans, and players serves another significant function: it democratises the sport. The vast array of inputs gathered aids in bridging the gap between top-tier professional settings and grassroots tennis. By leveraging AI to synthesise this collective wisdom, insights can be channelled overtly into mentoring programs, aiding young aspirants with data-driven guidance that was, until now, the preserve of those with access to top coaching methods. This underlines a shift towards inclusivity, with AI making complexity accessible to all.

AI-driven platforms have become matchmakers of sorts, aligning player profiles to potential tacticians or coaching styles, based on past performance data and player aspirations. Inputs from fans, encompassing discussions about epic rivalries or unforgettable matches, feed AI algorithms to form narrative patterns that offer players motivational touchstones. Through this, AI isn't just improving technical performance but enriching the emotive and psychological scaffolding around which players build their careers.

Feedback loops also play a crucial role in enhancing fan experiences, as AI can adapt broadcast content based on viewer engagement metrics gathered from diverse inputs. Algorithms analyse habits, preferences, and even dissatisfaction, modifying streaming options and interactive content dynamically. The AI systems then harness this data, providing a richer, more personalised comprehension of tennis, leading to a nuanced appreciation that might inspire deeper engagement or participation in the sport. This bidirectional flow from fans to AI, and back, cultivates a tennis culture that is both vibrant and inter-connected.

Another revolutionary aspect of fan and player inputs is their role in predictive analysis. AI doesn't only ponder on historical data from matches but also integrates spontaneous inputs from this community, crafting predictive models with unprecedented accuracy. Fans might notice nuances in a player's form on a particular day or identify anomalies that could indicate potential risks—all of which become data points that nourish AI models. Coaches and analysts can then tailor strategies mid-tournament, backed by the strength of crowd-sourced intelligence.

Engaging both fans and players in this ecosystem of intelligence gathering cultivates a sport that's perpetually evolving. This interaction with AI allows for shifts in tactics to be communicated almost like whispers shared collectively throughout the tennis community, ensuring that both the game and its followers grow in tandem. As AI continues to act as a conduit for these voices, the sport of tennis becomes not just a game of individuals but a celebration of collective endeavour and shared aspirations.

Open Data Initiatives

The sport of tennis, long reliant on instinct and tradition, is now embracing modernity through the power of open data initiatives. For the tech-savvy tennis enthusiast, these initiatives not only open a new frontier for understanding tennis but also push the limits of what's possible in terms of strategic insights and performance enhancement.

At the intersection of technology and tennis lies a vibrant ecosystem where data is not just collected, but shared and harnessed to drive innovation in ways previously unimaginable.

Open data initiatives invite a broader, more diverse group of individuals to contribute to the development and application of tennis intelligence. From amateur enthusiasts to seasoned professionals, these collaborative efforts provide the means to collectively analyse match data, identify patterns, and generate insights that transcend individual expertise. Whether it's through analysing player movements or understanding audience preferences, the scope of open data extends the analytical prowess of both players and coaches alike.

Beyond the immediate applications, the potential of open data is manifold. It serves as a bedrock for crowd-sourced intelligence—a concept where collective knowledge from tennis fans, analysts, and professionals is brought together to offer a richer and more nuanced understanding of the game. The democratization of data means that insights are no longer confined to elite circles. They become accessible to anyone willing to engage, analyse, and contribute, opening the doors to grassroots innovations.

These initiatives fuel an era where data is not merely consumed but actively contributed to. Take, for instance, platforms that encourage users to share their own match statistics, feedback, or even predictive models. Such participatory systems nurture a community of engaged fans and players who can draw on shared resources to enhance their personal and professional growth. This collective intelligence becomes a repository of tennis knowledge that continuously evolves, informed by real-world data and experiences shared by a global community.

Imagine a world where tennis enthusiasts can access a vast library of match analytics, vital statistics, and historical data at no cost. The implications are profound. Coaches have more tools at their disposal to craft strategies tailored to specific opponents. Players can leverage this treasure trove to refine their skills based on the success and failures of others. Open data turns every match into a learning opportunity, making training smarter and more efficacious.

One of the most enticing aspects of open data initiatives is the element of transparency they introduce. In a sport often criticised for its opaque decision-making processes, opening up data repositories allows for a more transparent and informed discourse. When data is shared openly, it fosters trust among stakeholders and fans, who can verify facts for themselves, engage in discussions, and propose alternative interpretations. This transparency bolsters the sport's credibility and invites a healthier dialogue about its future trajectory.

The utilisation of open data also paves the way for innovative applications yet to be fully explored. By making data accessible, new applications such as fan-driven analytics platforms and crowd-sourced coaching tools become not just possible but inevitable. These platforms can be used to simulate matches, predict outcomes, or develop training programs that adapt in real-time to player inputs. As more stakeholders embrace data sharing, the potential for creative and disruptive innovations becomes limitless.

Yet, tapping into the potential of open data is not without challenges. Ensuring data accuracy, maintaining privacy, and securing proper platforms for data sharing are essential components for the success of these initiatives. There must be a balance between open sharing and safeguarding sensitive information, ensuring that privacy rights are protected while promoting collaborative benefits.

Moreover, the landscape of tennis analytics is ripe for further exploration and investment. Establishing standards for data collection and sharing will facilitate the integration of disparate sources—creating an interoperable network of tennis knowledge. As more organisations and federations adopt these standards, unified efforts can lead to breakthroughs in programming infrastructures and analytical tools.

When players and fans come together to share and interpret data, they contribute to a deeper understanding of the sport's intricacies. This collective approach embodies the essence of community-driven knowledge, offering a tapestry of insights that would be difficult to achieve in isolation. The prospect of leveraging crowd-sourced intelligence in tennis is not just exciting—it's transformative.

Ultimately, open data initiatives empower every stakeholder in the tennis ecosystem to become an active participant in the sport's evolution. By fostering a culture of collaboration and transparency, these initiatives can reshape our perception of what tennis can be. They allow us to envision a future where artificial intelligence and human ingenuity coexist harmoniously, driving the sport forward in ways that honour its rich history while embracing cutting-edge technology.

In embracing open data, tennis becomes not just a game played on courts around the world but a shared journey toward enhanced knowledge, understanding, and appreciation of the sport. It invites every player, coach, and fan to be part of a dynamic conversation, ensuring that the intelligence gathered through these collective efforts continues to enrich the sport for generations to come. Together, through the lens of open data initiatives, the future of tennis promises to be as exhilarating as a championship match point.

The Collective Brain of Tennis

The landscape of tennis is rapidly transforming, unfolding as a dynamic playground for data-driven innovation. At the core of this evolution lies the concept of **crowd-sourced intelligence**, a collective brain that marries the wisdom of the masses with AI's computational prowess. This intricate web of shared knowledge enriches the sport by aggregating insights from diverse sources, including fans, players, and coaches, and feeding them into algorithms that refine every aspect of the game.

This concept sounds more futuristic than it really is. We've long relied on collective intelligence, albeit in more informal ways. Remember the countless discussions on online forums and social media, where fans dissect every aspect of the game—from player strategies to potential hack mechanisms? In bringing crowd-sourced intelligence into the fold, we're simply amplifying these natural behaviours with technology. *This* is where AI shines brightest, meticulously capturing and synthesizing nuances that humans might overlook.

Consider how this plays out in real-time match analysis. By tapping into the collective wisdom of a vast pool of tennis enthusiasts, AI systems gain a multitude of perspectives that enhance predictive modelling. When thousands of fans share their observations, and these are funnelled into intelligent systems, a more intricate understanding of match dynamics emerges.

In the realm of training, crowd-sourced intelligence enables unprecedented personalisation. Imagine a virtual coaching app armed with analysis from both professionals and amateurs around the globe, adjusting its recommendations based on an extensive library of player experiences. This transformation isn't just theoretical; it's happening now. Apps increasingly incorporate user feedback to refine their algorithms and deliver more accurate insights into training regimens.

Have you ever contributed to a strategy forum or shared a tennis clip on social media with your insights? Well, consider yourself part of this collective brain. The information you provide, however minor it might seem, could well influence the next set of algorithms developed for player training or match analysis.

While the expansion of collective intelligence networks offers exciting advancements, it also requires meticulous organisation of data. AI enables this through open data platforms, where information is collected, structured, and made accessible for tennis technology innovators. Open data initiatives are pivotal since they democratise access to high-quality data sets that were once siloed, ensuring that even smaller tennis clubs and budding startups have a seat at the table.

The challenges of curating this shared intelligence are non-negligible. There is a balancing act between gathering vast amounts of data and ensuring its accuracy and ethics. As AI systems interpret and utilise crowd-sourced insights, there's a high degree of accountability involved. Fortunately, the ongoing advancements in machine learning algorithms make it possible to detect anomalies and inaccuracies in the data, thus safeguarding its integrity.

Moreover, the collective brain isn't just an external force impacting the sport, but a vital interactive component where every participant has a role. Platforms that encourage both amateur and professional players to contribute their experiences help in educating novices and honing the skills of seasoned players. This shared pool of intelligence levels the playing field, offering insights that were once the privilege of those with exclusive access to top-tier coaches and facilities.

Yet, it's not just about creating a more technically skilled community of players. The emotional and psychological elements of tennis, often overlooked in traditional analytics, find a significant place in this model. The inclusion of fan perspectives can highlight emotional factors that influence match outcomes, such as the impact of crowd support on player performance.

It's crucial to recognise that the collective brain goes beyond current players and fans, extending to historical data as well. By integrating data from past matches and player performances, the collective intelligence model creates a richer tapestry of resources for

AI systems to draw from. This historical context adds another layer of depth to player analytics and strategy formation.

Another remarkable advantage of utilising crowd-sourced intelligence is its role in talent scouting and recruitment. Crowd insights, when processed by AI, can identify up-and-coming players by highlighting groundbreaking performances in lesser-known tournaments. This isn't just about finding the next star, but about fostering a wider appreciation of the sport itself, enhancing its global appeal.

Going forward, the tennis community is poised to further develop platforms for direct input from fans and players alike. *Imagine a future* where every match, comment, and observation you make contributes directly to a living system that's perpetually learning and evolving. This interaction creates a loop where AI learns from the community, and the community learns from AI, building a rich symbiosis.

And so, in the nuanced dance between technology and human insight, lies the future of tennis. As we venture deeper into the realms of crowd-sourced intelligence, the possibilities for enriching the sport multiply exponentially. By embracing the collective brain of tennis, we not only transform how the game is played but also how it is experienced by millions around the world. Through this synergy of human and machine, the sport finds itself on the cusp of a new era, where potential is only as limited as our imagination.

Chapter 25:
The Road Ahead

As we stand at the cusp of a new era in tennis, the future seems both exhilarating and challenging, filled with endless possibilities driven by artificial intelligence. The long-term vision for AI in tennis is not just about enhancing performance or refining strategies; it's about transforming the very soul of the game. As technology continues to evolve, we face intriguing challenges that demand creative solutions, from ethical considerations to the integration of AI in grassroots levels. At the same time, there's a tremendous opportunity for growth—how AI can bridge knowledge gaps, democratise access to advanced training tools, and inspire the next generation of players and coaches. The road ahead invites us to imagine and co-create a world where AI and tennis coexist symbiotically, advancing both the sport and our understanding of human potential on and off the court. With innovation as our guide, the journey promises to be as thrilling as the game itself, waiting for pioneers ready to embrace technology's potential while cherishing the timeless spirit of tennis.

Long-Term Vision for AI in Tennis

As we delve into the long-term vision for AI in tennis, it's crucial to acknowledge the profound shifts already set in motion. Artificial intelligence promises to usher in an era where the boundaries of potential, both on and off the court, expand like never before. The future landscape of tennis, equipped with AI, is a horizon filled with unmatched possibilities. Envision a world where AI not only complements training but also plays a pivotal role in shaping the strategies, ethics, and enjoyment of the sport.

At the heart of this future is personalisation. AI could transform how tennis players receive training guidance. Imagine each player's unique data footprint—spanning from performance statistics to biomechanical signatures—fueling tailor-made coaching programs. These AI-driven programs would be dynamically updated to account for a player's evolution, thus constantly priming them for peak performance. Such precise calibration could well redefine excellence in the sport.

Similarly, AI might redefine the dynamics of decision-making. Predictive analytics, capable of processing massive data streams instantaneously, would suggest strategic shifts during matches. Coaches would harness insights on opponent weaknesses, real-time player condition, and even the psychological state of the game to formulate tactical shifts. These real-time strategy adaptations could maintain the competitive edge, even under evolving match conditions.

A crucial aspect of AI's long-term potential lies in democratizing tennis. Leveraging AI, beginners in grassroots settings will access sophisticated training tools that once belonged exclusively to elite athletes. Smart rackets and AI-integrated courts might become standard fixtures, ensuring access to advanced play analytics. By balancing opportunities and maintaining competitive integrity, AI could level the playing field, inviting participation from diverse socioeconomic backgrounds.

Furthermore, AI is poised to make tennis a more sustainable sport. Energy-efficient smart infrastructure, optimised through AI algorithms, could minimise the environmental footprint of tennis facilities. Innovations such as AI-enhanced solar courts and intelligent energy management systems will align with global sustainability objectives, reflecting the sport's commitment to eco-friendly practices.

Beyond individual training and infrastructural impacts, AI's vision for tennis extends into fan engagement and viewing experiences as well. Fans could experience richer and more immersive content through virtual and augmented reality. Customisation options would go beyond personalised commentaries to deliver interactive experiences, such as choosing player-focused angles or accessing real-time stats overlays. AI-driven analytics could even predict match outcomes, adding a novel twist to the spectator experience.

However, amid these promising developments lie inevitable challenges. Ethical considerations remain at the forefront of AI adoption in tennis. Ensuring data privacy, preventing misuse, and upholding the integrity of the sport are paramount. As AI systems grow more sophisticated, governing bodies will need to develop and enforce regulatory frameworks that shield athletes' rights and maintain fair play. These frameworks would need to be dynamic, adapting to technological advancements while maintaining a steadfast commitment to ethical practices.

Inclusion and accessibility stand as another potential stumbling block. While advanced technologies often lead to cost reductions over time, initial investments may seem daunting, especially for clubs and players outside the wealthiest circles. Bridging this gap requires innovative models of collaboration between tech companies and tennis organisations, aimed at making AI tools widely accessible. It's about weaving AI into the fabric of tennis so that it elevates the sport holistically, rather than fractioning it further.

Ultimately, the long-term vision for AI in tennis is not merely about technological advancement; it's about integration into the sport's culture and ecosystem. Future generations of players, from juniors to professional ranks, will view AI as a natural ally in their development and career progression. AI won't replace the human elements of intuition, creativity, and esprit de corps unique to tennis; rather, it will augment these attributes, positioning players to achieve new heights of achievement.

The possibilities painted by AI in tennis are as exhilarating as a five-set thriller on Centre Court. Forging this future requires concerted efforts and shared visions across the global tennis community. Stakeholders, from players to coaches and fans to governing bodies, need to embrace AI's potential responsibly. This collective endeavour promises not just to enhance the game but to redefine what it means to excel, compete, and engage in the beloved sport of tennis. The journey to realising this vision may be complex, but the rewards of a tennis world reshaped by AI are worth the pursuit.

Future Challenges

As we look to the horizon of artificial intelligence in tennis, it becomes clear that numerous challenges lie ahead. These challenges are not merely hurdles to overcome but represent critical inflection points that will determine how AI reshapes the sport. While the possibilities are vast and promising, it's important to navigate the complexities with a cautious and informed approach.

One pressing challenge concerns data privacy. AI's remarkable capabilities are largely driven by vast amounts of data, often requiring personal information from players, such as biometric and performance metrics. In an era where data breaches and privacy invasions are hot topics, establishing robust protocols to safeguard player information becomes imperative. Balancing transparency and confidentiality will demand both technological innovation and ethical decision-making.

Furthermore, there's the question of fair play. AI, with its capacity for real-time analysis, could potentially tip the scales of competitive balance. As AI-driven insights become more accessible, there's a growing concern that unequal access could widen the gap between players from different economic backgrounds. Ensuring that AI benefits all players, not just the elite, is a significant undertaking that will require strategic policy setting and equitable access initiatives.

In addition to these challenges, the integration of AI in tennis could inadvertently shift how the sport is played and perceived. The authenticity of tennis – the human struggle, the raw emotions – could be undermined by over-reliance on technology. The art of intuition, once a prized skill, risks being relegated to the background in favour of data-driven decisions. This could fundamentally alter the fabric of tennis, making it an ongoing challenge to retain the essence and spirit of the game.

Another challenge involves the evolving landscape of AI technology itself. AI is a rapidly advancing field, and staying at the forefront requires continual upgrades and adaptations. Tennis organisations must invest in ongoing research and development to ensure that the technology they deploy remains relevant and effective. It's a race against time and technology, and falling behind could mean losing a competitive edge.

AI also raises pertinent questions around training methodologies. While AI-powered tools offer advanced insights and strategies, they could inadvertently pressure coaches to rely heavily on data, sidelining traditional coaching techniques. Finding a balance between utilising AI-enhanced strategies and maintaining human intuition and judgement will be vital for the future of player development.

Moreover, as AI becomes more integrated into the sport, there is an increased need for education and training for coaches, players, and support staff. Understanding how to effectively use AI tools and interpret the data they provide is no small feat. It requires new skills and mindsets, which could present a steep learning curve for some within the tennis community.

Regulatory challenges are also likely to emerge as AI becomes more entrenched in tennis. Sports governing bodies will need to establish guidelines to govern AI's use, ensuring it enhances rather than detracts from the game. This could span a wide array of considerations, from determining which technologies are permissible during matches to addressing potential disputes that arise from AI-generated decisions.

The financial aspect should not be overlooked either. Implementing AI systems can be expensive. Clubs and federations need to weigh these costs against the potential benefits carefully. More inclusive financial models and partnerships might be required to make these technologies accessible across all levels of play, from grassroots organisations to high-stakes professional tournaments.

Finally, the human element must always remain at the heart of tennis. AI can provide insights and predictions, but it can't feel the thrill of a match point or the anguish of a narrow loss. Preserving the emotional core of tennis, while harnessing the benefits of technological advancements, will be the ultimate challenge as AI continues to evolve.

In facing these future challenges, the tennis community has the opportunity to redefine what's possible. By addressing these issues head-on, balancing innovation with tradition, and ensuring inclusivity and equity, AI's role can be optimised to elevate the game for everyone involved. It's a visionary journey, one that promises to keep the sport dynamic, engaging, and ever-evolving.

Opportunities for Growth

As we look toward the future of tennis and artificial intelligence, the realm of possibilities seems almost infinite. This landscape that AI is helping to sculpt is dynamic, offering unparalleled opportunities for growth that can be harnessed by players, coaches, sports organisations, and technology innovators alike. The marriage of tennis and AI isn't just about refining existing processes but opening entirely new avenues for exploration and advancement.

One of the most exciting prospects lies in the potential to democratise access to world-class tennis training. Traditionally, top-level coaching and resources have been the privilege of a few, often limited by geographical and financial constraints. AI-powered applications, however, have begun to break down these barriers. They offer personalised coaching tips that rival in-person feedback, all through a user's smartphone or tablet. Imagine a young athlete in a small town having the same quality of training insights as those available to seasoned professionals in tennis academies. This levelling of the playing field can unearth hidden talents across the globe, creating a more diverse and competitive environment.

Moreover, AI presents an opportunity to refine and enrich player development programs at various stages. From juniors embarking on their first lessons to seasoned professionals looking to tweak their game, AI can provide tailor-made strategies that are continuously updated based on performance analysis. This adaptability offers a clear path for progression attuned to individual needs, making the journey from amateur to professional a tangible goal for many. Early interventions facilitated by AI tools can also mitigate the risk of chronic injuries, thus preserving player longevity.

Automation through AI could also revolutionise how we conduct tennis tournaments. With intelligent systems managing scheduling, player statistics, and even real-time error detection, tournaments could become more streamlined. This not only enhances the efficiency of event management but also improves the overall experience for players, officials, and fans. The resources saved from manual oversight can be redirected toward enhancing spectator engagements and promoting the sport at a grassroots level.

As AI continues to permeate the sport, data collection and analysis will become even more central to operations. This poses a significant opportunity in allowing coaches and analysts to make decisions that are informed by robust datasets. However, it is not just about the sheer volume of data but about actionable insights that can drive strategies. AI can detect nuances in player behaviour and opponents' tactics that the human eye might miss. This granular level of detail equips players and coaches with a strategic edge, potentially changing the outcome of tightly contested matches.

Beyond strategy, AI offers a platform for enhancing the mental aspects of the game. In the intense world of professional tennis, staying mentally resilient is as crucial as physical prowess. AI-supported mental conditioning tools can offer new techniques and insights into maintaining focus and composure under pressure. Machine learning models can simulate high-stress match situations, helping players to rehearse mental strategies as well as physical skills. This dual approach to preparation ensures that athletes are in peak condition for not only the physicalities of the game but its psychological demands too.

The burgeoning field of AI in tennis also speaks to fostering collaboration across industries. Tech companies, sports bodies, and academic institutions can join forces in research and development projects aimed at pushing the boundaries of existing technologies. This collaborative ethos beckons new business models and opportunities, inviting investment in research that could catapult both tennis and AI-engineering into innovative futures. Sponsorship and partnerships could proliferate, laying the groundwork for technologies that could be applied beyond sports, benefiting society at large.

Therein lies the opportunity for expanding educational outreach as well. As AI tech develops, there's a need to educate players, coaches, and even fans about how these tools can be used effectively. This knowledge transfer not only supports professional development but can also inspire the next generation of technologists and sports scientists, crafting careers at the intersection of AI and sports. Engaging youth in AI-based initiatives could spark lifelong interests and expertise in tech-driven careers, further closing the gap between technology and human interaction in sports.

As we stand on this precipice of change, the opportunities offered by AI in tennis also urge us to consider ethical implications and address concerns proactively. Building systems that prioritise fair play, data privacy, and integrity will be crucial as we navigate this novel landscape. It's about creating responsible AI solutions that complement human abilities and extend the spirit of sportsmanship that tennis so proudly upholds.

The road ahead, laden with these opportunities for growth, is one that champions both the advancement of technology and the sport of tennis. As AI continues to integrate more seamlessly into our sporting world, the potential for growth—player development, tournament execution, mental resilience, and global collaboration—is vast. Embracing these prospects with an innovative yet responsible approach will not only transform tennis but set a precedent for other sports to follow. It's an exciting time on the courts, where the possibility of redefining athletic excellence lies well within our reach.

Conclusion

The intersection of artificial intelligence and tennis has ushered in a new era, forged by the relentless pursuit of excellence and driven by the sport's innate dynamism. As we have journeyed through the intricate details of AI's impact on tennis, it's clear that this technology has not only revolutionised the ways players train and compete but has also reshaped our understanding of what's possible within the sport. AI has opened doors that were previously unimaginable, presenting a comprehensive toolkit that empowers players, coaches, and fans alike.

Tennis, often regarded as a game of strategy and physical prowess, now finds itself enriched by AI's ability to dissect and enhance performance. Performance analytics, once a manual endeavour relying heavily on observation and experience, have been exponentially augmented by AI. This shift has allowed players to refine their techniques with unparalleled precision and insight, transforming the way they approach training and competition. These advancements cater not only to the elite but also permeate through to amateurs and juniors, providing a scaffold for aspiring talents to bridge the gap to professional levels.

AI's role in training, particularly through tools like smart rackets and video analysis, has democratised access to high-level coaching. By personalising training regimes, AI has ensured that each player receives bespoke instructions tailored to their unique strengths and weaknesses. Coaches, too, find themselves benefiting from AI-driven insights, which enrich their strategies and enhance their decision-making processes. The collaborative nature of AI in coaching underscores its role as an invaluable ally rather than a replacement.

Moreover, AI's capabilities extend beyond the court, influencing the very infrastructure of tennis environments. Smart courts, equipped with IoT technology and automated systems, not only enhance the efficiency of match officiation but also optimise court management, contributing to a seamless sporting experience. Fans, often seen as passive observers, are now offered an interactive experience that engages them through personalised content and immersive virtual reality opportunities.

The ethical considerations that accompany AI's integration into tennis cannot be disregarded. As the sport becomes increasingly data-driven, questions surrounding privacy and fair play come to the forefront. Safeguarding data integrity while ensuring ethical compliance remains an ongoing endeavour, requiring vigilance from governing bodies and the broader tennis community. Nonetheless, with careful management and thoughtful regulation, the benefits of AI can continue to unfold without compromising these fundamental values.

Throughout this exploration, it's crucial to recognise that AI is never a standalone solution; it's an augmenting force that enhances the existing human element within the sport. The narratives shared by players indicate that AI's contributions are most effective when combined with the instinctual, emotional, and tactical nuances of human play. It's in this synergy between human creativity and computational might that tennis finds its true transformation.

Looking forward, the road ahead for AI in tennis is brimming with potential. With emerging technologies continually on the horizon, the landscape of tennis analytics is set for further innovation. Challenges relating to cost and accessibility will need to be addressed to ensure the widespread benefits of AI are shared across all levels of the sport. But with the continuous collaboration between tech companies, sports organisations, and the enthusiast community, these barriers can be progressively dismantled.

Tennis has always been a sport of evolution, adapting to new technologies and trends, and AI represents the latest, most profound chapter in this narrative. As we glean insights from other sports and incorporate player perspectives, the path becomes clearer, guiding us towards a future where AI is seamlessly woven into the fabric of tennis. The opportunities for growth are immense, and the potential for AI to effect positive change throughout the sporting world is limited only by our imagination and commitment to this transformative journey.

Appendix A: Appendix

In the dynamic landscape of tennis, artificial intelligence is not just a tool; it's becoming an integral partner that reshapes the way we perceive, play, and appreciate this classic sport. This appendix provides supplementary insights and additional context to support the main text, highlighting the intersection of technology and tennis like never before. From a technical evolution that's transformed our understanding of baseline plays to the nuanced data analytics driving player improvements on and off the court, AI is the silent force behind the scenes, whispering strategies and enhancing every serve and volley. Here, we've compiled additional resources for tech-savvy enthusiasts eager to delve deeper into this revolution, offering guidance and direction for further exploration in an ever-evolving AI landscape. While the book has focused primarily on high-level strategies and innovations, the appendix serves as a reservoir of knowledge, encouraging enthusiasts to become pioneers of AI-driven tennis ingenuity and impact. Our combined efforts empower a new era of tennis where the human spirit is constantly uplifted by the intelligent algorithms shaping tomorrow's champions.

Glossary of Terms

In the rapidly evolving world of tennis powered by artificial intelligence, a comprehensive glossary of terms is integral to understanding the myriad of concepts and technologies driving this revolution. Here, we've curated a list of essential terms that will enhance your grasp of the intersection between AI and tennis.

Artificial Intelligence (AI): A branch of computer science aimed at creating machines capable of performing tasks that typically require human intelligence, such as learning, problem-solving, and pattern recognition.

Biometric Tracking: The use of technology to monitor physiological and movement data from athletes, providing insights into health, performance, and improvements through devices equipped with sensors.

Data Analytics: The science of analysing raw data to make conclusions about that information, used extensively in tennis for performance metrics, match strategies, and player development.

Internet of Things (IoT): A network of physical objects embedded with sensors, software, and other technologies, facilitating data exchange over the internet. In tennis, IoT enables smart courts and real-time feedback.

Machine Learning: A subset of AI that involves training algorithms to improve automatically through experience and data utilisation, crucial for predictive modelling in tennis.

Predictive Modelling: A statistical technique leveraging historical data to predict future outcomes. In tennis, it can forecast match results or player performance trends.

Smart Rackets: Rackets integrated with sensors that gather data on swing, stroke, and impact, offering detailed analysis to improve player techniques and strategies.

Virtual Reality (VR): A computer-generated simulation of a three-dimensional environment that can be interacted with in a seemingly real way by a person using special equipment, enhancing fan engagement in tennis.

Wearable Devices: Portable devices that athletes wear to collect data on physical activities, biometrics, and more, instrumental in tailoring training and improving performance.

This glossary serves as a foundational reference for navigating the exciting developments AI brings to tennis. As you delve deeper into the chapters that follow, these terms will be pivotal in understanding how technology continues to redefine this beloved sport.

Additional Resources

For those keen to delve deeper into the enthralling intersection of tennis and artificial intelligence, there is a treasure trove of resources available that can elevate both understanding and appreciation for the game's transformation. From online courses to cutting-edge software, and insightful podcasts, these resources cater to a wide spectrum of interests and levels of expertise.

One of the foremost resources to consider are online platforms offering courses and tutorials on AI and its application in sports. Websites like Coursera and edX host comprehensive courses run by top universities. These courses can help you grasp the fundamentals of

AI, machine learning, and data analytics—tools crucial for decoding performance metrics and enhancing coaching strategies.

In addition, books authored by experts in the field provide an academic yet accessible examination of AI's burgeoning role in sport. Titles such as "AI for Sports" by Christer Bodell and the "Handbook of Artificial Intelligence in Sport" edited by Tim B. Levermann offer a thorough dive into technological advancements influencing modern tennis. These works not only debate the utility of AI but also explore ethical concerns and future possibilities.

To experience AI tools firsthand, several software applications are designed to assist players and coaches with performance analysis. Applications like SwingVision, which use AI for real-time shot tracking and instant video analysis, are indispensable tools for tennis enthusiasts striving for improvement. Using these applications elevates one's game by providing tangible data and insights that can transform on-court strategies.

Podcasts serve as another engaging way to stay updated with the latest trends and expert discussions. Shows like "The AI in Sports Podcast" bring together athletes, data scientists, and experts to engage in lively discussions on how technology is remaking the sport. Listening to these discussions not only informs but also inspires, supplementing your learning journey with personal anecdotes and success stories.

For research-oriented individuals, academic journals and conference papers are a vital source of insight. Publications like the "Journal of Sports Analytics" feature peer-reviewed articles that explore innovative AI implementations in sports contexts. These technical publications delve into case studies and experimental methods that reveal the scientific foundations of transformative technologies.

Engaging with the tennis community is also invaluable for shared learning and networking. Online forums and social media groups can connect enthusiasts and professionals who are eager to discuss the implications of AI in tennis. By exchanging ideas and experiences, these platforms foster a communal knowledge base, vital for the sport's growth and innovation.

Furthermore, many tech companies and sports organisations host webinars and live discussions to discuss the latest in AI technologies tailored for tennis. Attending these events can provide exclusive insights into upcoming innovations and practical demonstrations of AI tools in action.

Museums and exhibitions dedicated to the history and future of tennis, such as the International Tennis Hall of Fame, often showcase interactive exhibits that highlight technological advancements. These exhibits can be both educational and experiential, offering a tactile sense of how the sport has evolved with AI innovations.

In professional settings, attending conferences such as the Sports Analytics Conference or the Artificial Intelligence and Machine Learning in Sports Forum can provide unparalleled opportunities to learn directly from scholars, industry leaders, and influencers pioneering AI applications in tennis.

Within the realm of player development, AI-driven platforms like PlaySight offer highly sophisticated analytics for consistent progress tracking and performance evaluation. Utilising these platforms can bridge the gap between raw talent and polished skill by leveraging data to optimise techniques and reduce injury risk.

For a more structured and systematic approach to learning, university degrees specialising in sport science or data analytics offer focused modules on sports technology and AI applications. Such programs are ideal for those aspiring to integrate AI solutions professionally within tennis organisations.

Finally, volunteering or interning with AI tech companies working in the tennis sphere can provide firsthand experience. This practical immersion aids both career growth and personal understanding, allowing you to be a part of an exciting era of innovation in tennis.

Empowered by these additional resources, one can not only comprehend the potential of AI but also actively contribute to its advancement within the world of tennis. Whether you're a player, coach, analyst, or enthusiast, these tools and communities await to fuel your passion and expand your horizons.

Printed in Dunstable, United Kingdom